FOREWORD

We are limited to this world--the only world that we can examine. We cannot fly to some other planet or into some other dimension to find answers. We are limited to the present. We cannot borrow knowledge from the 22nd century. We must come to conclusions that are based on the present as have other thinkers in the past. We must move from the known to the unknown. So if we do not ignore the evidence from the totality of man's experience and if we do not allow ourselves to get side-tracked into discussing the PROCESS, there should be, based on the evidence, only one answer to the question of God's existence.

This book gives solid logical and scientific evidence to back up this conclusion.

GOD

IS

GOD

SPOKE

GOD

CAME

Rev. Ralph E. Cox

Apologetics with a heart: Simple but compelling
evidence for God, the Bible and Christ designed to
bring agnostics to faith in Christ.

DEDICATION

"My father used to jokingly say that all missionaries should be allowed to have three wives--one to assist in evangelism and church planting; one to be his secretary to care for the voluminous correspondence; and one to be a faithful wife and mother. God in his mercy gave me all three in one--my wife, Stella, who has faithfully served by my side for over 40 years. This book is gratefully dedicated to her."

ABOUT THE AUTHOR

Rev. Ralph E. Cox was converted to Christ while serving in the United States Navy during World War II. He holds a B.S. degree in accounting and an M.A. in theology. He and his wife, Stella, have served as missionaries in Japan for 44 years under the auspices of The Evangelical Alliance Mission (T.E.A.M.). Their entire ministry has been in church planting and evangelism mainly in Western Japan where they are presently still serving.

The contents of this book represent the basic approach that Ralph has used in bringing hundreds of Buddhists, Shintoists, atheists, and evolutionists to a firm faith in Jesus Christ. It is designed to give you information that will enable you to answer the critics doubts and move on to a presentation of Jesus Christ as their Savior.

Through their more than 40 years of ministry they and those working with them have started over 55 churches. Forty of these churches are completely self supporting, fifteen are in various stages of development and most have their own land, buildings, and Japanese Pastors. From this work 60 Japanese have gone into full-time Christian service — 5 to the foreign mission

About The Author Continued

field and 45 American young people (short-termers) have returned to Japan as career missionaries.

God has used the unique apologetic approach explained in this book to help accomplish the above. Laying a foundation in men's hearts for a faith based on evidence has brought stability, confidence, and permanency to their wide-spread ministry.

In His glorious service,

Ralph E. Cox

PREFACE

Moving to Japan to confront Buddhists, Shintoists, and others with the Gospel of Jesus Christ was an unnerving experience. The Japanese people are highly educated. They are not only steeped in their own religions but thoroughly educated in evolutionary, atheistic science. Although I was firmly convinced of the power of the Gospel to convert and change men of all cultures, I knew that easy answers would not suffice in Japan. How could I refute the arguments of educated Buddhists and Shintoists as they intelligently defended their own beliefs? Could I in good conscience continue to proclaim Christ as the only way in the face of their arguments?

My first five-year term, though blessed in many ways, was mainly spent learning the Japanese language, their religion, and their culture. The main accomplishment of my first term, though we saw a new church established, was probably (through much study, prayer, and discussion with Japanese religionists and atheists) the solidification of my conviction that the Bible and its message are unique and true.

It was during this five-year period that I gained confidence to speak to anyone, regardless of how well educated, concerning the truth of the Christian faith.

Preface Continued

This came about through first understanding that all religions, including atheism, start from the same point--FAITH. They all BELIEVE certain basic things. Therefore, in comparing belief systems, we need to examine the type of faith required. Is it a blind, superstitious type of faith, or is it an objective faith based on verifiable evidence--a scientific faith?

Faith leading to a knowledge of fact and truth must be based on evidence, objective and provable. It is precisely at this point that Christian faith makes its departure from the other belief systems of the world and lays its claim to being unique. The key word in comparing the different faiths of the world is EVIDENCE, just as evidence is the key word in separating scientific truth from superstition.

This book will logically present the evidence that supports the three main pillars of the Christian faith:

1. God is (Creator)
2. God spoke (Bible)
3. God came (Christ)

The majority of this book, however, will examine evidence for the existence of God; if God does not exist, the other two points cannot be true.

Preface Continued

For years, those who have heard this presentation have requested that I put it in writing. God has finally given me time to do just that during four months of recovering from a severe operation. I have written this book with a strong conviction that it will strengthen your own faith and give you practical information on how to witness to atheists and evolutionists. It is a book that you can give to your skeptical friends to bring them face to face with the reality of God's existence and, hopefully, to faith in Jesus Christ. It largely removes evolution as a barrier to faith.

The final preparation of this manuscript was made possible through the kindness of Dr. Louise Bentley who sacrificially gave of her time and talent to correct the grammar and sentence structure. Her many helpful suggestions have also been incorporated into the final manuscript.

TABLE OF CONTENTS

Part I

GOD IS

(*The Creator*)

Chapter One

THE RIDDLE

For 44 years, as a missionary to the Japanese people, I have presented the Gospel to thousands. The Japanese are highly educated. They are not only steeped in their own religions but thoroughly educated in evolutionary, atheistic science. Almost everyone I witness to comes with the following assumptions:

1. There is no God.
2. Man is his own God.
3. Evolution is a fact of science.
4. Religion is only for weak people.
5. Christianity is only another religion.
6. Faith is only a psychological crutch.

Many Americans have almost the same set of beliefs. Therefore, the purpose of this book is evangelistic--to present logically to an atheist or a non-Christian the evidence that supports the three main pillars of the Christian faith (God, the Bible, and

Jesus Christ) and to lead them to saving faith in Jesus Christ.

In witnessing to an atheist who strongly believes in evolution, the discussion will inevitably deteriorate into an argument about evolution. In this book, I have presented an effective way to avoid this argument and get to the main point--whether there is scientific evidence to support the existence of God.

I personally do not believe in evolution as commonly taught. But in witnessing to these people, I explain that even if evolution were true (God could use any of a thousand different ways to make man.) it would be only an explanation of the way (the process) that God used to make man. It does not explain what caused this process. Instead of discussing the process, this book concentrates on the main question: Is there a God and where is the evidence to prove it?

Most non-Christians in America are familiar with the creation story in the first three chapters of Genesis. As evolutionists, they feel that Genesis contradicts the findings of science and is only a myth. Many Japanese don't know the Bible, and initially are unaware of these conflicts. However, as I witness to them and as they begin to read the Bible, these conflicts arise.

Since the purpose of this book is evangelism--to lead atheists to faith in Christ, I try to avoid the controversies that surround the various interpretations of the first few chapters of Genesis: Are the days 24-hour days or long periods of time? Is the earth only a few thousand years old or billions of years old? Arguing these points only leads away from the main purpose of the discussion--to lead an atheist to belief in God and then to salvation through Christ.

In order that his evolutionary views not be a stumbling block to further discussion or to faith, I try to show that TIME is not a problem with God. He could have created everything in one second, in six days, or in trillions of years. If He created everything in one second, it would still appear to man as if it had to have taken a tremendously long time.

I try to emphasize that the main purpose of Genesis 1 is to show WHO made everything and to reveal the order in which He made it. The time factor is secondary, so we should not get side-tracked in that discussion.

In witnessing to atheists, I have, on many occasions, been able to avoid arguing about evolution or about the time frame of evolution as opposed to the time frame of Genesis. Postponing these topics for later discussion enables me to concentrate on the key points and sometimes lead an atheist to accept Christ in only one sitting.

Other times it has taken many sessions of frank discussion, focusing only on the main points. Of course all do not accept Christ, but by avoiding questions that lead away from the main points, I am able to show that the primary barrier to faith is not lack of evidence. They may break off the discussion, but deep in their hearts they leave knowing that lack of evidence is not the problem. The real problem is an unwillingness to believe, <u>regardless of the evidence</u>. This is because man is a sinner and doesn't want to believe.

Please remember as you read this book that its main purpose is to give information that will lead evolutionists and atheists to Christ. Once the Holy Spirit has come into a person's life through faith in Christ, evolution and the time frame of Genesis are not insurmountable problems. Therefore, I try to help them over these stumbling blocks so that we can concentrate on the heart of the matter--**GOD IS; GOD SPOKE; GOD CAME**.

DOCTOR SUZUKI

It was past midnight and Dr. Suzuki's wife had already gone home to look after their two little girls. Over the past several months, I had been answering their questions and explaining God, the Bible, and Christ to them.

"I believe," exclaimed Dr. Suzuki, " I am now ready to accept Christ!"

"Wonderful!" I replied. "Your wife has been ready to accept Christ for at least a month but has been waiting for you to decide. Call and ask her to come back here so that you can together pray to accept Christ as your Savior."

Dr. Suzuki immediately phoned home and told his wife of his decision. Within a few minutes, she was sitting with us in the living room of my house. Once more, I went over with them God's plan and provision for their salvation and asked, "Do you now confess that you are sinners, that Christ died, was buried, and the third day rose from the grave to save you from eternal punishment for your sins?"

"Yes, we do," they responded in unison.

Together, we opened our Bibles to Rom. 10:13 and they read aloud, "For whosoever shall call upon the name of the Lord shall be saved." Then they bowed their heads and asked God to forgive and save them through Jesus Christ.

Dr. Suzuki was a very intelligent, well educated 34-year-old medical doctor practicing in one of our nearby hospitals. He was a family oriented man who loved his two daughters. The eldest had become ill and the doctors could not find the problem. Week by week her condition deteriorated. One of our workers asked permission to pray for her, and God apparently healed her. Almost immediately she began to improve and has not since been sick. Because of this and the insistence of one of his friends, he and his wife started attending my Friday night Bible study sessions for non-Christians.

Dr. Suzuki was never belligerent but had very openly declared himself an atheist who felt that evolution explained everything and belief in God came only from superstition and the desire of mankind for some super being. In his mind, God did not make man; man invented God.

By answering the Suzukis' questions and presenting the evidence contained in this book and through "closet prayer," God gradually opened their eyes to the truth. They accepted that God exists and that the Bible is His word. Lastly, they accepted its message concerning Christ, and on that memorable night became children of God. About a month later, they were baptized and began their walks as witnessing Christians.

My ministry in Japan as a church-planting missionary is basically pioneering--starting churches where there are no churches. This means that I am constantly presenting the Gospel to people such as Dr. Suzuki who have never heard. The people that I contact are educated Buddhists, Shintoists, atheists, and agnostics.

Buddhists and Shintoists in Japan are basically pantheists believing that the totality of nature is God. They worship trees, mountains, people, water, and all other parts of nature because the indwelling spirit of all these is god. A large number, however, while following the duties required by their religions, are atheists or agnostics.

The first step in trying to reach these people for Christ is to help them understand that there is a transcendent God separate from His creation, that He is the maker of all things, that He actually exists, and that there is ample evidence to prove this. I often open a discussion of this subject by posing the following riddle:

THE RIDDLE

Let's suppose that all of us were born in your house and lived together until the present. Let's suppose that your house doesn't have (never has had) any doors or windows. In other words, the inside of your house is all that we know or ever have known. We cannot see outside, and nothing from outside ever penetrates your house.

We would wonder what is outside--or even if there is an outside? We would discuss among ourselves whether there were other houses like this with people like us living in them. Some would contend that we were all there is; others would firmly believe that there must be other places just like this. We would speculate about the unknown.

THE QUESTION

Is there any possible way that we could know that someone besides us exists? Think about it for a moment before you continue to the next paragraph. Remember, there are no doors or windows, and nothing from outside penetrates.

There is only one way that we can really know that anyone else exists. We can argue among ourselves, guess and speculate, but that will never result in sure knowledge. The only way we can know for certain that a person or persons besides us must exist is to look at the abundant evidence that surrounds us.

In every room of the house we see furniture, light fixtures, and plumbing. We did not make these. They were there when we were born in this house. They are too intricate, too perfect to have just happened. They are all composed of smaller parts-- systems within systems. Someone with intelligence had to make them and place them in this house for our use. They could not have just happened all by themselves.

Judging from the evidence--the plentiful evidence in every part of the house--someone else has to exist. That is all we have to guide us. All else is guesswork, pure speculation. All the fixtures in the house serve as evidence that clearly points to the existence of at least one other intelligent being besides us.

In this riddle, the house without doors or windows that all of us are born into is this world--our universe. For us, it has no doors or windows. Nothing from outside penetrates it. The strongest telescope cannot even reach its boundaries--or does it have boundaries? Our telescopes and most advanced scientific instruments cannot look beyond our universe to see if there are other universes out there. The universe, for us, is a doorless, windowless dwelling place. We are born into this house, our universe, and from childhood we wonder if there are other universes like it. We wonder if we humans are the only ones here or if there are others like us somewhere out there. We wonder if there is a maker that we call God or if all of the wonderful things around us just happened. We argue, guess, speculate, and often come to no firm conclusion. Can we really know?

Chapter Two

BIBLICAL EVIDENCE FOR GOD

"For the invisible things of him from the creation of the world are clearly seen, being understood by the things that are made, even his eternal power and Godhead; so that they are without excuse:" Rom. 1:20

This verse clarifies all the principles stated in the previous riddle:

1. We live in a world that is wonderfully prepared for us.
2. The one who prepared this world for us is not visible or evident.
3. He has, however, left proof of His existence through all the things that He has made--things so superior to anything

man can make that there is no comparison.

    a. These intricate systems are seen in the cosmos, in inorganic minerals, in all plants, animals, and humans, and are evident to all.

    b. Each of the hundreds of complete systems (a bird, a bee, a tree, a man, an atom, an amoebae, etc.) is composed of hundreds of other unbelievably intricate, minute systems.

4.   We can, then, conclude not only that He exists but also that:

    a. He is living;

    b. He is extremely intelligent;

    c. He has great power; and

    d. He cares for us because He provides for our needs.

5.   Anyone who denies the bountiful evidence of an intelligent being behind these intricate systems condemns himself because

a. The totality of man's experience proves that only intelligent beings can produce systems;

b. Systems never come into being by themselves.

We will deal with the basic principles discussed here in a later chapter. It is sufficient to say that Rom. 1:20 is the main argument presented in the Bible for the existence of God, and this argument is repeated throughout the Bible. For example:

> "The heavens declare the glory of God; and the firmament sheweth His handiwork. Day unto day uttereth speech, and night unto night sheweth knowledge. *There* is no speech nor language, *where* their voice is not heard. Their line is gone out through all the earth, and their words to the end of the world." Psa. 19:1-4

The Bible offers "the things that are made" as the main evidence of God's existence because this argument is conclusive and is available to all mankind. A later chapter will deal with this evidence from a logical and scientific point of view.

When the atheist stands before God on that great judgment day, I can imagine a conversation such as this:

> *God*:   Why didn't you believe in me?
>
> *Atheist*:   Because I could never see you or find you through any scientific investigation.
>
> *God*:   I am a Spiritual being, and scientific processes have not advanced to the point of being able to investigate the spiritual realm. Didn't you see all around you the beautiful and intricate systems that I made?
>
> *Atheist*:   Yes, but I thought that all those things just happened by themselves.
>
> *God*:   Just happened by themselves? Did you ever experience one system--even a very simple system--that happened by itself? Man has made millions of systems. Did any one of those just happen? All systems existing in nature are

far superior to any system man has ever made. So how could you think that all man-made systems (inferior systems) came about only through intelligence but that far superior systems could happen spontaneously?

Atheist: SILENCE

(Because as Rom. 1:20 states: in the face of the evidence of creation, anyone who does not recognize that an intelligent and powerful being is the originator of everything will stand before God "without excuse.")

Chapter 3

UNDERLYING PRINCIPLES OF SCIENTIFIC INVESTIGATION

Science has progressed to its present high level of respect because of its strict adherence to certain basic principles. Strict adherence to these principles has enabled science to separate itself gradually from error--myth, superstition, and false beliefs. Most of mankind at one time believed that the sun rotated around the earth, that the earth was flat, that life was spontaneously generated from decaying substances, that the microscopic world did not exist, and that various myths and superstitions were true. Thanks to science, most of mankind is now free from these errors.

The highly developed technology of today's industrial world has come about mainly through the scientific process. Christians need not be afraid of true science. We benefit from it in many ways and should be thankful for it. Our Christian belief system follows the same basic principles that underlie science, and it is this fact that separates Christian faith from the belief systems of the world.

       True science starts with a set of assumptions that cannot be proven but appear to be true. It then operates from a set of principles that are basic to its procedures.

BASIC ASSUMPTIONS:

1. The world around us is real.
2. We have only our reasoning power to lead us to fact/truth.
3. The laws of nature are not capricious--they will be the same tomorrow as they are today.

PRINCIPLES:

1. Separation from subjectivity (separation from feelings, biases, prejudices, etc.)
2. Adherence to objectivity (seeing what really is--reality, fact)
   a. Gathering of evidence

       b. Comparing evidence with evidence

       c. Drawing conclusions based on this objective evidence

       d. Obtaining verification by unbiased third parties

I have not included "FAITH" as one of the basic principles underlying the scientific process because scientists do not include this as one of the basic principles for all science. Instead of using the word "FAITH," science uses the word "CONCLUSION." What they are really saying is, "Based on the evidence, we believe (conclude) certain things are true" (principle 2.c.). So it is very important to understand that FAITH (CONCLUSION in science) is one of the basic principles underlying the whole scientific process. Not only Christians need faith but all scientists need faith. Let me explain:

A few hundred years ago, almost all scientists, based on the evidence available to them, concluded (believed) that the earth rotated around the sun. This was their firmly and widely held conclusion (faith) based on the "facts" of science.

In the not-too-distant past, most scientists believed that life was generated spontaneously from decaying matter. This was the conclusion based on actual observation. These same scientists also concluded (believed) that the microscopic world did not exist.

In the early 1960's, most scientists throughout the world concluded from their studies and from the evidence available to them that man would someday be able to ride a rocket to the moon. This conclusion, though not at that time proven, was firmly held (believed). It has since been proven. Their conclusions (faith) have been verified. Today many scientists also believe that someday man will walk on Mars. This may or may not happen, but it is the conclusion (faith) of most scientists drawn from the evidence.

When I was in high school, I was taught that matter can neither be created nor destroyed. Based on Newtonian physics and abundant evidence, scientists all over the world had theorized that the elements making up the universe could change their form, but the basic elements were fixed--their number would always remain the same. This belief (conclusion), though held by many scientists, was modified by

Einstein and others of his generation. The conclusion (belief) of present day scientists is that matter (elements) can be converted into energy and thus no longer exist as elements. This knowledge gave birth to the atomic bomb.

In other words, theories (conclusions) formulated from experimentation and the observation of various phenomena are believed until further evidence confirms them or dictates their abandonment or modification.

In every age, differing theories on various subjects are held by sincere scientists. Conflicting conclusions are often drawn from the same evidence. Scientists believe, with varying degrees of confidence, a certain conclusion (theory) until evidence supporting a different theory becomes so abundant and strong that the new theory demands acceptance (belief).

Many other modern examples could be given, but the above-mentioned should serve to show that FAITH (conclusion) mentioned in 2.c (drawing conclusions based on objective evidence) is one of the basic principles of the scientific method. In this world we can seldom have 100% proof. Therefore, we and scientists must draw conclusions based on the evidence--in other words, **believe**.

This is also the foundation of everyday life. When a friend promises to meet us downtown, we go there and wait by faith. When we order merchandise and give our credit card number to a company, we have concluded (believed) the company will keep its word. This is not blind faith, rather faith based on evidence. Sometimes we act with very little evidence and are deceived.

In all fields of science, some theories are very firmly believed because of ample evidence, while others are believed for a short time but quickly abandoned when conflicting evidence increases. In this world, since 100% proof is scarce, conclusions (faith or beliefs) will always be necessary for all mankind (including scientists).

Another important principle underlying the entire scientific process is COMPARISON--comparing evidence with evidence (Principle 2.b previously listed). Only through this process of COMPARING evidence with evidence and then BELIEVING what the evidence indicates has science progressed. In the face of new evidence, scientists through the ages have modified or abandoned or further confirmed strongly held theories and so-called "facts of science."

Chapter 4

ANATOMY   OF   SYSTEMS

A SYSTEM is a device composed of separate parts logically organized so that they function together to accomplish a specific purpose.

Millions of systems exist around us--in nature and in those that man has made. We come into contact with them everyday. We can study them in great detail and have done so--both natural systems and those that are man-made. Man-made systems exist from the simple to the complex.

My illustration of this range in complexity is from a fingernail clipper to a powerful computer--one of the most complex systems that man has ever developed. In nature, systems also exist from the simple to the complex--from the atom to man's brain, the most complex   system   existing   in   nature.   When we investigate all the systems that man has made, we discover that they have, <u>without exception</u>, come into existence through exactly the same three steps:

1. All systems <u>that we can investigate as to their source</u> started as an idea in the mind of some living, intelligent individual.

2. This individual, using his intelligence, devised a process that would produce the system that he saw only in his mind. After initiating the process, he then actively guided that process with his intelligence and power and caused it to become the system that he had envisioned in his mind.

3. The finished system exists on its own--completely separate from its maker--ready to perform the task for which it was designed.

At this point in our examination, the importance of remembering these three steps cannot be over-emphasized. They apply to ALL man-made systems (the only systems that we can examine as to their source). Millions of these systems exist and have ALL been produced by the same three steps from earliest man to the present. You can look at any of these systems and know that at one time each of them existed only as an idea. They were not physical entities but ideas in someone's mind.

This person then, to give his idea reality, devised a process to guide his system to completion. He started with simple bits of material, fashioned them into the desired form, and gradually assembled them into increasingly complex forms. When he had completed this process, he could stand proudly gazing at the system he had brought into existence. He and all other human beings know that this system existing before their eyes came through three steps:

1. **IDEA**--intelligent thought
2. **PROCESS**--steps of development
3. **SYSTEM**--finished product.

As we begin to investigate the systems existing in nature--living and non-living, organic and inorganic--we soon discover that all are far more complex than any system man has made. Even the simplest systems found in nature are far superior to any system man has produced. The depth, the intricacies, and complexities of each astound even the greatest minds. Astronomers probe the depths of the grand system that is our universe, and their discoveries are even beyond their great intellects.

Biologists have moved from understanding the anatomy of plants, animals, and man to a discovery of the complex DNA from which all of these are formed. They have discovered that DNA codes exhibit vast libraries of "knowledge"--and still their investigation probes even deeper.

The nuclear physicist, probing the depth of the atom, which just a few years ago was thought to be the ultimate basic building block (the simplest form of all matter), has now discovered within it still smaller "particles" to investigate.

In these three fields of science, the more deeply scientists probe, the more complex they discover these systems to be--so complex that human intelligence can hardly grasp what is being revealed by the investigation. Only a handful of the greatest minds in the world are able to comprehend what is being discovered in all three disciplines.

If we measured all systems (man-made as well as natural) on a scale of 1 to 100 (from simple to complex), we would undoubtedly find that man-made systems would occupy only the first digit or so on the scale. All systems found in nature, by comparison, would fall between 90 and 100. The extent of this gap in complexity and depth can hardly be measured.

All systems that we are able to investigate <u>as to their origin</u> started as ideas in the minds of intelligent living beings. Add to this the fact that the most complex and intricate systems that man has been able to develop have been possible only through the accumulated knowledge of all generations from the beginning of man.

Brilliant minds today are able to develop extremely complex systems only because they are able to borrow intelligence from the great minds that have gone before them. The accumulated intelligence of our generation is a result of mankind's being able to preserve the knowledge of all ages and utilize it to develop modern, complex systems. Yet, man-made systems are so far inferior to nature's systems, there is no comparison.

In light of these facts, known by all modern-day scientists, how can so many of them conclude that there is no intelligent being behind the universe? The answer is the THEORY OF EVOLUTION (most scientists would say, "FACT OF EVOLUTION"). Evolution, it is thought, explains everything. If we are, therefore, trying honestly to seek evidence for the existence of God, we cannot exclude a discussion of the evolution theory.

The purpose of this book is not to critique the theory of evolution but to eliminate it as a barrier to faith; consequently, the theory of evolution will be discussed only AS IT RELATES TO THE SUBJECT OF GOD'S EXISTENCE.

EVOLVE and EVOLUTION simply mean, "to change." In this sense of the word, probably none of us would dissent. If the word today still signified only "change," we could all call ourselves evolutionists.

We all recognize change in the animal and vegetable kingdom. Selective breeding continually produces changes from the original. This is clearly evident among dogs. Selective breeding has produced so many varieties of dogs that because of size and other factors, interbreeding is now impossible in many cases. They are, nonetheless, still dogs.

The national flower of Japan is the chrysanthemum. Through selective breeding, there are now so many different varieties of these flowers that some bear little resemblance to a chrysanthemum. None of them, however, have ever become roses or any other flower.

It is Darwinian evolution and the various theories of evolution stemming from it that many Christians, including myself, find unacceptable. This type of evolution (also called macro-evolution), where one living creature changes gradually into a completely different creature, is based not on proof but on faith. This has never been demonstrated but is assumed that it can and did happen. We exist in our present form, so "HOW ELSE COULD IT HAVE HAPPENED?" This is the question that evolutionists ask.

We need to emphasize that evolution, even if true, explains only the PROCESS that produced all living things. We, however, are not discussing the process but the source. Evolution does not answer the question, "What caused the process?"   Therefore, whether true or false, evolution is unrelated to the question of God's existence. God certainly used some PROCESS to create man, whether He did it in 24 hours or in a billion years.

For this reason it is very important that we don't allow ourselves to get side-tracked into discussing the merits of the evolution theory. That is a scientific question and should be left to the specialists. We, in a sense, don't care what PROCESS God used. It is immaterial to the question of God's existence. We need to keep the discussion centered on the issue of God and the evidence that supports our belief in His existence.

An intelligent being is behind every system that we can investigate as to its source. In every case, intelligence guides the process, so even if the evolution theory is true, it still needs an intelligent being to guide it into producing man.

For further study, please see the Bibliography for books written on the defects of Darwinian evolution by scientists and scholars who are not convinced of its validity.

Chapter 5

EVIDENCE FOR GOD'S EXISTENCE

In discussing the existence of God, it is important to understand that there are only two possible answers--either He is or He is not. One is wrong and one is right. All mankind stands under the same heavens and is surrounded by all of nature. As they observe all of this, some conclude that it just happened and that God does not exist. Others are convinced that there has to be a Creator.

These are two theories of origin, one true and one false. There is no middle ground, so let us logically and scientifically examine these two conflicting theories to see where the evidence points.

Regardless of which we believe, a voice out of heaven will not declare one correct and the other wrong. We have no judge to come forward with a final verdict. As in all other questions of science, we must assemble the evidence supporting each theory; compare evidence with evidence; try to remove ourselves from all bias and prejudice; and then draw a conclusion based solely on the evidence--in other words, BELIEVE what the evidence dictates. This is a position of faith for both the atheist and the theist but, as will be shown, the evidence supporting the theistic position is conclusive.

Systems exist in nature, but we have no means to investigate their source. We can examine the source only of man-made systems, and 100% of them came about through the same three steps. There are no exceptions to this rule.

THE THREE STEPS:

1. **IDEA:** All systems start as ideas in the mind of a living, intelligent being.
2. **PROCESS:** This person then develops the process that will produce the system.
3. **SYSTEM:** Finally the completed system exists independently of its maker.

This is the experience of all mankind (100% of mankind). This is the proven result from the examination of all systems (100% of systems) <u>where we can confirm their source.</u> We cannot confirm the source of systems that exist in nature. We desire to do so, but presently there is no way that we can do so. Whether we like it or not, we are limited to the data at hand--systems whose source we can examine. Therefore we must draw conclusions from the known, as scientists have always done. To do otherwise is to revert to pure speculation. That is not science.

When I talk to atheists and agnostics (and I have talked with thousands), I explain that when I want to buy a watch I am not interested in HOW it was made but rather that it was made by a reputable company. I am interested in the maker, not the PROCESS that it went through to become a watch. A watch maker will probably be interested in the PROCESS. When I purchase a car, I am not interested in the PROCESS but in the finished product and the company that made it.

In talking with atheists and agnostics, we Christians often allow ourselves to be side-tracked into a discussion (argument) about the PROCESS (step 2 in the development of any system), when rather we should be discussing the SOURCE--the originator (step 1). We should not be particularly interested in the PROCESS. God could have chosen a thousand different ways to make man. Let's leave the process to scientists who are interested in investigating the HOW of the question.

To prevent being diverted into a discussion of the PROCESS, I, though not an evolutionist, for the sake of the discussion and to get back to the main point, concede that the process WAS evolution. God could have used that method, so let's save that discussion for some other time.

Let's focus instead on whether it is even remotely possible for a system to develop without a maker. Our conclusion must be drawn from the evidence. Let's admit (for the sake of argument) that the PROCESS of human development was evolution. Then ask, "What caused the PROCESS?"

This approach removes evolution, a diversion, from the discussion of the principal subject. It is much like trying to lead a smoker to Christ and getting into a long argument over the evils of tobacco. Tobacco is not the main subject; his accepting Jesus Christ is.

The question remains: "Is it possible for a system to develop without a maker?" The totality of mankind's experience in investigating all systems that we can examine as to their source answers clearly, "IMPOSSIBLE." This conclusion stems from the evidence--All mankind's experience = 100%; All systems = 100%. Without exception, these systems all went through the same three steps:

1. **IDEA** of an intelligent being;
2. **PROCESS** guided by this being; and a
3. **SYSTEM** existing independently of that being.

An atheist believes that steps 2 and 3 are sufficient to explain the wonderful systems existing in the world around us. On the basis of what evidence does he believe this? The answer is NONE. He just believes it without a single example of its ever happening. He believes that all inferior systems need an intelligent maker, but far superior systems can happen by themselves. He believes in an unbelievably great effect without an equivalent cause.

It is as if I, a male, suddenly proclaimed, "Although I know that throughout history only women have been able to have babies, I believe that I can, too!" You would immediately ask, "On what basis? Has that ever happened?" I would answer, "No, but I believe I can!"

Let me emphasize that there can be only two possible answers to our question. One is right and one is wrong. The only possible means that we have to find the correct answer is to draw conclusions from the systems that we know. What else is available to us?

We are limited to this world--the only world that we can examine. We cannot fly to some other planet or into some other dimension to find answers. We are limited to the present. We cannot borrow knowledge from the 22nd century. We must come to conclusions that are based on the present as have other thinkers in the past. We must move from the known to the unknown. So if we do not ignore the evidence from the totality of man's experience, and if we do not allow ourselves to get side-tracked into discussing the PROCESS, there should be only one answer to the question of God's existence <u>based on the evidence.</u>

Let me illustrate:

"YES"	"NO"
(CHRISTIAN'S BELIEF)	*(ATHEIST'S BELIEF)*

based on

100% OF MANKIND'S EXPERIENCE	"0" EVIDENCE
100% OF SYSTEMS	

The atheist believes that <u>only</u> a process is sufficient to explain the superior systems in nature <u>without even one</u> example of such ever happening. This is neither logic nor science but blind, superstitious faith. He can only revert to discussing the PROCESS--not the real point of our discussion. We all admit that there had to be a process, but that is not the basic issue, and we need continually to bring the discussion back to the main point. The PROCESS can be dealt with later, as a separate subject.

I have never met an atheist who has been able to answer this logic. Once the unrelated discussion of the PROCESS is removed, the poverty of his position is exposed and he has nowhere to flee. This, as I have explained, is the argument of Rom. 1:20. It is sufficient and is just as the verse states--anyone who does not recognize the evidence of the magnificent systems that God has made is "without excuse" because the evidence is conclusive.

Many times when I have talked to atheists with open hearts, I have been able in only one sitting to move on to the next two points--God spoke (the Bible) and God came (Jesus Christ), and in some cases pray with them to accept Christ.

Chapter 6

PROBLEMS ATHEISTS
MUST FACE

In this chapter, I would like to present one more strong argument for the existence of God and also discuss other bits of "evidence" that atheists present to try to bolster their position.

CHANCE EVENTS

In our world we experience many "chance" events as well as carefully planned happenings. An earthquake, a volcanic eruption, a violent hurricane, and an explosion--all come under the category of "chance" happenings--events not planned by an intelligent human being. Each time they occur, the results are different. We can study them, but we cannot precisely predict what is going to be destroyed or what the results will be.

Planned happenings--a jig-saw puzzle, a watch, a bridge, or a hydro-electric plant-- can all be studied by other intelligent beings and can be gradually understood. Because they can be completely understood, they can be duplicated. What one intelligent human produces, no matter how complicated, can eventually be understood and reproduced by other intelligent beings. This cannot be done with chance happenings.

The evolutionist will often state that scientists are gradually unraveling the secrets of nature and that someday they will even be able to create life. Occasionally, they state that science will, given enough time, be able to explain everything. God does not have to be part of the equation. This argument used to disturb me greatly, especially the fear that some scientist might actually discover how to create something that is living.

Later I understood that of course scientists should be able gradually to unravel the secrets of nature. They are studying the planned happenings of an absolute being. What one intelligent being makes, another studies, understands, and also duplicates.

Since intelligence is behind all of creation, it would be strange if man could not study and understand it.

If life is something CREATED by God, we should expect that scientists, given enough time, may be able to understand it and duplicate it. However, if life is something directly imputed--something that is a part of the very life of God--man will never be able to duplicate it. It may, however, be something similar to electricity that we have learned how to generate.

A "chance" happening is the only one thing that man cannot understand and duplicate. For instance, if I tore a book into tiny pieces and dropped them on the floor, you might observe the shapes and pieces and how they lay, but it would be impossible for you to rip an identical book to shreds and duplicate the exact patterns and shapes. Since there is no intelligent thought behind such an exercise, it simply cannot be understood and duplicated.

Therefore, when the atheist uses the argument that God doesn't exist because scientists will eventually be able to explain everything, he is not following the evidence. Scientists are studying the very objects that intelligence has brought into existence so, of course, they should be able to understand and explain them. If they study random happenings, occurring only by chance, the evidence says that they cannot understand and explain them.

The fact that they <u>can</u> is evidence for God's existence, not the opposite. If science through centuries of study could completely understand all of nature and the universe and all laws that governed it and could then duplicate all that is in the universe, they have not proven that God does not exist but that GOD IS. If I study a watch, understand it and then duplicate it, have I proven that the watch has no maker? How illogical!

SCIENCE CANNOT FIND GOD

Sometimes atheists will try to support their position by stating that science can find no trace of God. Of course that is true. Scientists have not yet progressed to the point that they can test the existence of a spiritual realm. Perhaps in the future they will discover how, but at this juncture of scientific development, they have found no trace.

What if scientists of past ages concluded that the microscopic world did not exist because they could find no trace of it? Gravity, light waves, radio waves, etc., have been discovered only as science has progressed. So the fact that science has not discovered God is certainly no evidence that He is not. Undoubtedly, there are many things existing all around us right now that scientists have not yet discovered.

Things that cannot be seen by the naked eye are the most difficult to discover. They are usually discovered by the effect they cause because the effect can often be discerned. Newton's apple led to the discovery of gravity, and the consequences of germs led to the discovery of the microscopic world. The effects (a magnificent creation) of the invisible God should thus lead to acceptance of His existence.

EVIL AND SUFFERING

Because evil and suffering exist, many people find it difficult to believe that an omnipotent, all-knowing God really exists. This does not prove that God does not exist. If we look at the world around us, we see that all is not evil. Good also exists. Therefore, judging from the effects evident in the world, there must be not only a cause of evil but also a cause of good.

The Bible explains why God has allowed evil. It further states that all good comes from God and evil from Satan and sin. Satan's origin is explained, and the

Bible promises that when all of God's purposes are fulfilled, Satan, sin, and evil will be completely eliminated from God's perfect kingdom. The existence of evil, therefore, does not prove that God does not exist but that a source of evil (Satan) must also exist.

WHERE DID GOD COME FROM?

Many will at this point ask, "Where did God come from?" or "Who made God?" There are a number of possibilities, but I will comment on the three most probable answers.

1. Perhaps the God of our world was born (or made) from another God and He from another, and so on. Regardless, of how far back you extend the chain of Gods, you still face the question of where that first God came from.

Atheists face the same problem starting with energy. Where did it come from? Even if they discover some new source for energy, the question of the origination of that source will still remain.

Consequently, atheists usually assume the eternity of energy--it always was.

2. Perhaps a group of "gods" planning together made everything. This is a logical possibility, just as #1 is logically possible.

Both #1 and #2 have many examples in our world and so must be dealt with as possibilities. Here again, we have not solved our problem because the question of where these gods came from is still unanswered. Therefore the eternity of something has to be assumed.

3. Another possible answer is that God was not created or born from some other God but always existed. He is eternal--without beginning or end. He is an absolute being. He is the source of everything and always was.

Christians, while admitting that #1 & #2 are logical possibilities, reject them because the Bible repeatedly and very clearly states that there is only one

God, and He is eternal. The Bible claims to be a revelation from this eternal Spirit, and it gives abundant evidence that it is what it claims to be. Therefore, from faith based on this evidence, we accept answer #3--God is eternal--He always was and He is only one. (Science is forced to a similar conclusion concerning energy--that it is eternal.)

SUFFERING CAUSED BY CHRISTIANS

Pointing out the defects of Christians and Christianity--the Crusades, Christian wars, and such-- is a last-ditch attempt to move the discussion away from the main point. This is simply a smoke screen to avoid acknowledging the evidence for God. These discussions have no connection to whether God exists. Such arguments only show the defects of Christianity and that Christians do not always obey God.

Logically God could exist and not even be the God of the Bible. He could exist and be a limited God or even an evil God, so this argument should be recognized for what it is--another diversion. Reasons why we believe Him to be the God of the Bible will be discussed in the chapter entitled GOD SPOKE.

Chapter 7

GENESIS AND THE THEORY OF EVOLUTION

Even in countries with Christian backgrounds, evolution is taught as a fact in science classes and through the media. It is loudly proclaimed as the only possible position of educated people. Anyone who is not an evolutionist is not considered academically credible. He is like those who believe in a flat earth.

In most other countries, including Japan, where we have spent our lives as missionaries, this is also true. However since Japanese have no knowledge of the Bible, they feel no conflict between the teachings of the Bible and their belief in evolution. The subject matter of the preceding chapters helps them to see that God actually exists and has led many to accept Christ. It, however, does not deal with the problem of evolution as it relates to the Bible. When new Christians read the first few chapters of Genesis, this problem arises, so as early as possible in their Christian growth, I help them to resolve these difficulties.

My purpose is not to convert them to my personal position but to help them see that Genesis should not be a barrier to faith. This chapter will explain the method I have found to be most effective. Later I have them read books written by competent Christian scientists (and there are many) who believe the Genesis account and do not believe that the scientific evidence supports evolution. Many evolutionists have never read such a book.

Most non-Christians in Western cultures have a knowledge of the Bible, and many already believe that the "facts" of science and the first chapters of Genesis cannot be reconciled. Since this will invariably be part of the non-Christian's argument against accepting the God of the Bible, we need to deal with this subject as part of our discussion on the existence of God.

In this chapter, I will not be presenting only one interpretation of Genesis but rather giving information that will help a seeking evolutionist see that Genesis need not be a barrier to faith in God, the Bible, and Jesus Christ.

Dedicated, Bible-believing Christians themselves are vastly divided on the interpretation of the first few chapters of Genesis. The following views of Genesis Chapter 1 are held by various Christians throughout the world who clearly state that they believe in an inerrant and infallible Bible:

a. Evolution can be reconciled with the Bible because the Bible does not explain how God created.

b. The days of Genesis are vast periods of time.

c. The days of Genesis are 24-hour days.

d. The days of Genesis are 24-hour days marking the end of long periods of creative activity between each day. Each day merely delineates the end of a new creative act.

e. The first two verses of Chapter 1 are NOT part of the first day. The first day starts from verse 3. Verse 1 tells of the creation of the whole universe including sun, moon, and stars. Verse 2 describes the condition of the earth before God's creative work ON EARTH starts in the third verse.

f.   Verse 1 tells of an original creation and between verses 1 and 2, the original creation was destroyed by some chaotic event such as the fall of Satan. Verse 2 explains the desolate condition of the earth before God created once again, starting from verse 3. All the geologic ages took place before verse 2, so most ancient fossils were probably part of the timeless original creation.

g.   Calculating from the genealogies and time frame of Genesis, the whole universe and all that is in it cannot be more than 10,000 or so years old.

h.   The universe may be billions of years old, but the six days of creation on this earth took place only a few thousand years ago.

i.   God created a finished product in six days. Therefore trees, rocks, man, and everything else appear old to scientists but are actually young. In this view, the fossils are usually placed between verses 1 and 2 (as explained in "f") or as a result of the flood.

j.   To make things look as if they were old would be a deception on God's part, something He would never do.

k.   Genesis was never intended to reveal a definite time frame but only to show who made everything and the precise order of that creation.

FACT #1

God, in revealing beginning events, was faced with the problem of presenting an account of creation that would be factual and yet could be understood by people of all ages, from the most educated to the most illiterate. He also chose to limit Himself to explaining all the astounding events of creation from the very beginning down to the creation of man IN ONLY ONE SHORT CHAPTER. Those are tremendous limitations. Therefore, we have an extremely condensed, but accurate, outline of all that happened.

FACT #2

Nowhere in Genesis 1 does God explain how (THE PROCESS) He did all that He did. It merely states that He did it. It is like saying General Motors made a car or Bulova made a watch. Neither statement explains how.

FACT #3

The material utilized to make all that we see around us is not explained except in the case of man. Genesis Chapter 2 states that the material used for man was "dust." A theistic evolutionist would interpret this to mean that, starting on day three, God made man via the route of evolution from inanimate substances. Only inanimate substances existed until day three. Most who accept a literal 24-hour day believe that God made Adam from inanimate material in just one day.

FACT #4

The order of events in Genesis 1 broadly follows the same general order taught by evolutionists, especially if the interpretation of view "e" is followed (all Heavenly bodies including the earth were created in Gen. 1:1). When we get into the fine points and details, we find this, of course, is not true. Evolutionists, themselves, are divided on the fine points and the exact order of progression. They, therefore, would not find much to quibble about in the order of events listed from Genesis 1:

- creation of the whole universe including sun, moon, and stars
- earth shrouded in darkness
- water in atmosphere
- light diffused over the earth
- division of waters above (in cloud cover) and below (in oceans and land)
- vegetation
- sun, moon, and stars made visible from earth
- fish, birds
- large land animals and "creeping things"
- man

FACT #5

God is eternal--He is not limited by time.

"...One day is with the Lord as a thousand years, and a thousand years as one day." (II Pet. 3:8).

God did not need six days to create everything. He could have done it in one second. Or if He had chosen to take trillions of years, He still would have had plenty of time left.

FACT #6

If God in only six days created a mature and perfect creation, there would be absolutely no way that man could detect this. Everything, no matter how carefully scrutinized, would give the appearance of age.

One of the basic assumptions of science (note Chapter 4) is that the world around us is real and that it reveals reality. When a scientist sees a mature tree and other objects, he can only assume a lapse of time. When he sees a cosmos stretching out billions of light years, he can only assume a great lapse of time. Otherwise science is no longer science.

This dilemma will never be resolved. A scientist must believe what He sees; therefore, to discuss the time frame of Genesis is immaterial. According to Einstein's theory of the relativity of time, when we get to heaven we may find that six literal days of creation and billions of years are both correct in God's dimension.

FACT #7

No one was there when God created; therefore, scientists as well as theologians must interpret from the available evidence. Since both are prone to error, neither should be dogmatic. More important than the time factor is, "Who did it and in what order?" These matters are clearly stated in Genesis 1 and basically agree with scientific thought.   Besides explaining the foregoing facts, it will help the seeking atheist or evolutionist to reemphasize the following:

1. Bible-believing Christians differ in their interpretations of Genesis Chapter 1.

2. Future studies of many excellent books from a variety of Bible-believing authors will help guide him to his own interpretation as he grows in the faith.

3. The teachings of Genesis are no real barriers to faith.

Chapter 8

AN INTERPRETATION OF GENESIS 1

This interpretation purposely tries to follow present scientific thought on the order of creation as much as possible because we are dealing with those who are coming from that perspective. Accordingly, it follows the interpretation held by many dedicated Christians--that the whole universe was created in verse 1, and God's creative activity on earth started with verse 3.

Where scientific thought contradicts the order taught in Genesis, the Genesis order is always followed. There is no merit in opposing scientific interpretation of the evidence from nature just because it comes from scientific investigation. On the contrary, we should seek to come to the same interpretation whenever possible, as long as it does not violate Scripture. Otherwise we may find ourselves in the same position as earlier Christians who believed that the Bible taught a flat earth and that the sun rotated around the earth. They had to correct their interpretation of the Bible as scientific evidence to the contrary mounted because the Bible did not teach what they thought it did.

In explaining Genesis one to a person who has lived for many years as an atheist or agnostic, I try to present it in a way that will be most easily understood by him. Therefore it may seem that I have adhered to a billions-of-years plan for the days of creation. This is not true. In this interpretation, I have attempted to avoid the TIME element. Therefore either a literal six-day or a billions-of-years explanation will fit.

Jesus instantly turned water into wine and made withered arms whole. He instantly multiplied five fish and two loaves and fed over 5,000 people. Instantly, God made Aaron's dead rod bloom and bear fruit. Hence, He certainly could have done everything in one instant, in six days, or in trillions of years. As you read, therefore, do not consider a TIME factor.

> "In the beginning God created the Heaven and the earth." Gen. 1:1

Man had lived on this earth for thousands of years before Genesis was ever written and thus was familiar with the heavenly bodies and all of nature. In Genesis, God is explaining to him and to all future generations where the heavenly bodies, the earth, and all that is in it came from. He is saying, "the heavens that you see, I made; the beautiful earth that you live on, I also made. These were the very first things that I did in preparing your habitation." In this interpretation, it is important to remember that the sun, the moon, and the stars are all created in verse 1. In other words, "heaven" means "universe."

"Earth" is singled out for special mention because God is speaking to people who live here. If He were writing for people who live on Mars, then Genesis 1:1 would probably read, "In the beginning God created the heaven and Mars." If He were writing to people on Jupiter, then He would probably say, "In the beginning God created the heaven and Jupiter" because they would be familiar with only Jupiter. Since He is writing to us, He emphasizes "the earth," our dwelling place.

Man was very familiar with a beautiful and abundant earth. This is the only earth that man has ever known, so in verse 2, God is explaining that it had not always been so. In verse 2 He seems to be saying that if you lived on the earth in the beginning, you would see nothing that resembles the earth you have known. In fact, you would be shrouded in darkness, and all around you would be no familiar form to which you could relate. However, throughout the watery atmosphere, God's Spirit would be working to bring about this beautiful world. In a sense, man is standing with God on the earth in the very beginning and listening as God explains the creative acts that brought about the world with which man is familiar. In interpreting the rest of Chapter 1, it is important to remember that the point of view is earth-centered. In fact, from Genesis 1:2 to the end of Revelation, God is speaking to an earth-bound, earth-centered humanity. He is telling us all that we need to know.

In verses 3-5, God tells man as he stands, so to speak, on the formless earth in pitch-black darkness that the first thing he would see would be light penetrating the darkness as God thinned the thick cloud coverage. This light would be diffused over the whole earth, generating 12 hours of day and 12 hours of night. "I made that light," God is saying.

On the second day (vs.6-8), God created what we commonly call sky--the space between the waters beneath (which on day three became oceans) and the vast amounts of water stored in the cloud coverage for rain, snow, etc. (Some believe that excess amounts were stored there until Noah's flood.) If man were present at that time, God is explaining, he would have witnessed this further progression toward man's familiar world.

On the third day (vs.9-13), God made the oceans, continents, and the vegetable kingdom. If man had been there, he would for the first time recognize familiar sights and would begin to feel "at home."

On the fourth day, God is explaining, "I made the Heavenly bodies, which until now have been invisible to you and to all else on earth." Actually they were created in the very beginning but only made visible for earth-centered man on the fourth day when the cloudy atmosphere was completely removed and clear skies appeared.

The sun, moon, and stars created in verse 1 were not yet visible to man (had he been there) because of the thick misty atmosphere still surrounding the earth. This was removed on the fourth day. If man had been on the earth during the first, second, and third days of God's creation, he would have moved from darkest night to a dawning of full day (the fourth day). During day three He would be standing in bright light diffused over the whole earth with a light cloud cover still overhead preventing his seeing the Heavenly bodies.

If vehicles that can fly above the clouds had not been invented and if every day was a cloudy day, the sun, moon, and stars would not exist as far as we could discern. We would have no idea what existed above the cloud cover and what caused 12 hours of light and 12 hours of darkness. As far as we could know, there would be no sun, moon, and stars.

On the fifth day, God created moving creatures in the waters of the earth and flying creatures in the sky. Evolutionists, in discussing Genesis Chapter 1 with Creationists, will point out discrepancies between the order generally accepted by evolutionists and the creation account of what God did on the third and fifth days. These difficulties are about the finer details of just what happened on these two days and what evolutionists believe to be the order of development.

A number of books deal with this problem, so I will not try to resolve the difficulties here. Broadly speaking, there are not great difficulties. Evolutionary thought is not united on the exact order; it also changes. Christian interpretation of exactly what these verses are saying is also not unanimous.

We can say with confidence, however, that in both Genesis and in the teaching of evolution, water and land preceded the vegetable kingdom; the vegetable kingdom preceded fish and birds; fish and birds preceded large land animals; and large land animals preceded man.   Beyond that, the details will vary according to interpretation.

We should also remember that the evidence of past events remaining in nature is very sketchy at best. The account in Genesis of all of God's creation in one short chapter has to be unbelievably brief. Therefore, dogmatism should be avoided; discretion should be the rule.

The creation of animals, and lastly of man on day six, does not present any special problems that need to be dealt with here, but we do need to emphasize that man and only man was a special creation in the image of God.   Man alone has a God-consciousness and is capable of fellowship with God. In fact, the difference between man and all creatures below him is so great that even evolutionists do not really know how to explain it.

To illustrate this, I often ask whether there is a greater difference between a mouse and the highest apes, or a greater gap between these apes and man.

Most people, judging only from body size, will answer the former. However, I am convinced that other than body size, the gap between man and primates is by far the greatest. Mice and primates, though differing in brain capacity and body size, are governed mainly by instinct. Both do basically the same things throughout their lives--care for their young, forage for food, and strive to protect themselves. None of the higher qualities of man are even faintly discernible in either. Think it over!

Chapter 9

THE CHRISTIAN AND SCIENTIFIC THOUGHT

As Christians, we should not be afraid of scientific investigation. Almost all great scientists to the middle of the eighteenth century, and even later, felt that they were exploring God's creation. Only through scientific investigation were they discovering how God caused certain things to happen. They believed that an intelligent being was responsible for all of creation. In other words, they believed that God is an intelligent being and therefore another intelligent being (man), though greatly inferior, through diligent study and investigation could gradually understand what God has done. They considered themselves only thinking God's thoughts after Him.

For example, most of us are not watch makers, but by intense, careful study of a watch, we could begin to understand how it functions, the relationship of the various parts, and the principles that govern it. Eventually we could make a similar watch.

In the same way, scientists have through diligent study grasped the principles of much in nature. Early scientists could not understand how birds, which are heavier than air, could fly. They now understand and, by applying the same principles, can make heavier-than-air objects fly. Our artificial satellites mimic satellites in nature.

Different from their predecessors, many scientists today start with the assumption that God does not exist. Everything must be explained through "natural processes" without any intelligence to guide it. It is this assumption that Einstein could not accept. He saw evidence of intelligence in the whole of nature and could never declare Himself an atheist, even though He never accepted the Judeo/Christian God.

As Christians we should not fear scientific investigation that asks the question, "HOW DID GOD DO IT?" instead of the question, "HOW DID IT HAPPEN?" Newton, one of the greatest scientists who ever lived, along with most great scientists of his day, conducted all their investigations from this perspective.

We exist in our present form and, as Christians, believe that an intelligent being created us. Therefore there must be a way to do it. If we were as intelligent and powerful as God, then we also should be able to make a man. We do not know how, and even if we knew, we lack the power to do it. Since there is a way to do it, just as there are ways to make satellites, heavier-than-air flying objects, and hearts that mimic real hearts, is there any reason that a Christian scientist should not try to understand how God made us? He may never be able to decipher this riddle, especially if it resides only in the spiritual realm, but he can at least try.

We are trying to unravel God's secrets in almost every realm of nature and to use this knowledge to advance civilization. Just as we, through study, can discover the secrets of a watch, Christian scientists can gradually discover some of the secrets of God's great watch called the universe. There is nothing wrong with this type of consecrated investigation.

Since we do exist and since God made us, trying to explain HOW is what science is all about. Granted, the answer may never be discovered, but scientists can try to find out and pass on to the next generation any knowledge gained in that and other fields. The next generation can apply that knowledge to solving other problems.

The atheistic evolutionists ask, "HOW?" To answer, "God did it," is really no answer. This, though true, does not make any attempt at explaining HOW. The evolutionist challenges the Christian with the question, "If evolution is not the way it happened, then what is a better explanation?"

Dedicated Christian scientists should accept that challenge, especially since the Bible nowhere explains HOW. It just says that He did it. In the case of Adam and Eve, the Bible explains the material that they were made from but it does not explain HOW God made them.

Through investigation, scientists can now explain the "how" to many mysteries of past ages. Further investigation of the HOW question as it relates to man will undoubtedly result in better explanations that are more in accord with Genesis. God did it, and so there is a way to do it though we can never discover how.

Even now, in trying to explain man, some evolutionists have rejected the gradual change theory and accepted a theory of sudden and radical jumps to a totally different creature. These radical steps or jumps, they believe, fit better with the fossil record. They cannot explain the mechanism of such; however, it better fits the record in Genesis than does the gradual change theory.

Astronomers through the "Big Bang" theory now believe that in the first few seconds of time, the whole cosmos expanded into existence. This theory also is much closer to the teaching of Genesis 1:1. If scientists would accept the fact of God's existence, they would realize that God could easily have created in one day what appears to man to have taken much longer. This would focus attention on the question of "HOW," regardless of how long it took. The two groups would thus find themselves much closer in their thinking. The Bible does not explain, "HOW," so dedicated Bible-believing scientists should, through their studies, be able to gradually narrow this gap.

"COP-OUTS"

1. As explained, Christians "cop-out" when they answer the evolutionists' questions concerning the how of our existence by the simple answer, "God just did it." That

avoids any attempt to answer "HOW." This, rightly, annoys the evolutionists. This answer and this attitude have led some of the more extreme evolutionists to state that God cannot be a part of science.

In making this claim, they ignore the views of earlier scientists. Great scientists of past generations discovered the "how" of many baffling questions such as: What is the foundation of the earth? What keeps earth-bound objects from flying into space? What causes diseases?

They did not just answer, "God did it"; they offered explanations. That is what the evolutionist is asking of Christians. It is far better to answer, "I don't know," than to use a "cop-out." We can further explain that true science, given time, will likely arrive at partial answers that will undoubtedly concur with Genesis.

2. Christians are not the only ones who "cop-out." When asked what causes the mechanics of evolution, the atheistic evolutionist usually answers, "It is just an inevitable law of nature; it is through 'natural processes.'"

The word "nature" or "natural" are "cop-out" words used to answer a question that we do not know how to answer. When a small child asks how babies are made, many parents, not wanting to go into an explanation of sex, will explain that when two people get married they naturally have children. That is a "cop-out."

"Why does an apple drop?"--the question that troubled Newton, and all other questions of science, could be answered by explaining that it just naturally happens. That is a "cop-out." When they can explain, scientists do not use these words.

Since the atheist denies the existence of God, he is forced to use a "cop-out" word in order to avoid the obvious conclusion that there must be a guiding intelligence behind all--an explanation that agrees with the evidence. He knows this, and he knows that the upward progression of matter without the intervention of some outside force contradicts the second law of thermodynamics--entropy. (Simply put, this law states that everything tends toward decay, not orderly progression.) But what else can he say except, "There is a God who must have intervened to cause orderly progression in creation."

God-denying scientists following the "Big Bang" theory believe that energy was condensed into an extremely small ball containing all of the present elements in the universe. It exploded and expanded into our present universe and, through mindless evolution, became all that is.

The Christian need not shy away from the "Big Bang" theory, except the "mindless" part. Even six literal days to create the entire vast universe and all of nature was certainly a "Big Bang." Just think of the tremendous explosion and expansion that had to take place--almost instantaneously--to create all that is. That is certainly a tremendously big and fast "bang."

In explaining the "Big Bang" of creation, the Christian view is far superior: In the beginning, only an eternal, living, intelligent, powerful Spirit existed--and nothing else. Through His own intelligence and power, this Spirit (God) created (spoke into existence) the energy that He caused to change into compressed elements. He then caused these elements in one "big bang" of creative activity to become our vast universe (millions of light years in diameter) and all of nature, including man--whether He did it in six days or in a trillion years.

This makes sense because intelligence is controlling everything--not mindless energy or matter. It is logical and follows the proven steps that all other systems have followed.

The major difference between an atheist's faith and a Christian's faith is that an atheist believes everything evolved from eternal, mindless energy. A Christian believes that everything was created by an eternal, intelligent, powerful Spirit.

In other words, the energy that apparently made everything was not first. It has no intelligence. A living, intelligent, eternal Spirit was first, and energy came from this Spirit (God). The scientist needs to go back one more step in time and there he will find God, the eternal one. This fits the evidence.

This brings to a close our discussion of the evidence that supports the first pillar of Christianity--GOD IS. We will now turn briefly to a discussion of the second pillar--GOD SPOKE.

Part II

GOD SPOKE

(The Bible)

Chapter 10

SOURCES OF RELIGIONS

Let's return to the riddle that we stated in the beginning of Chapter 1. We were all born into a house without doors, windows, or any access to the outside world. We have lived there all our lives, and nothing can penetrate from outside. The inside of the house is all that we know. We don't even know if there is an outside. We wonder if there are other places like this and if anyone exists besides us.

In Chapter 1 we determined that we could know that at least one other person existed: the one who prepared the house for us. The house is filled with furniture, a water and electric system, kitchen equipment, etc. These things could not have happened by themselves; therefore, someone besides us must exist. All the fixtures and equipment in the house prove His existence.

We do not know, and have no way of knowing, but outside our house is a whole world filled with people, homes, highways, oceans, and mountains. Our house has no doors or windows and nothing can penetrate from the outside.

THE SECOND QUESTION OF OUR RIDDLE

We would speculate about the unknown, but, "Is there any possible way that we can learn about the wonderful world existing outside our home?" Think about it. Is there a way?

There is only one way, and that is if the person who furnished our home and prepared it for us informed us about the outside world. We could guess, speculate, and propose various theories, but we could be certain only if someone who knows about the outside world explained it to us.

But could we trust the transmission? There is no way for us to go outside and check the accuracy of the message. Maybe it is just fiction--a fabrication. How can we be sure?

If the explanation relates only to the outside world, there is no way that we can verify its contents.

However, if the transmission talks in detail about two realms--the inside world (our home) and the outside world--then the details of our home and events that have happened in it can be verified. If they are extremely accurate, they give grounds to believe that the details of the outside realm are also accurate. If they are inaccurate, why should we trust the explanation of the outside realm?

This riddle explains the gulf that separates Christianity from the religions of the world. Almost all religions claim to have knowledge about life after death, the spiritual realm, God, the purpose of life, where we came from, and where we are going. All this, in a sense, is about facts that lie outside our realm of existence--outside our house (our universe). Knowledge of these facts is, therefore, dependent on REVELATION.

Almost all religions (atheism would be an exception) claim revelation from an outside source--God, angels, spiritual messengers, those who have died, or other sources. How can we discern which to believe? This is mankind's dilemma. This is why so many different religions survive. How do these religions differ? How can we decide which one to believe?

First of all, we need to consider the possible sources of these "revelations." There are at least six:

1. God and His angels
2. Satan and His angels
3. Neurosis
4. Drugs
5. Self-deception and hypnotism
6. Purposeful fraud

1. GOD AND HIS ANGELS:

In the first part of this book we gave abundant proof for the existence of God. The Bible claims to be a revelation from God.

> "God, who at sundry times and in divers manners spake in time past unto the fathers by the prophets, hath in these last days spoken unto us by His Son..." Heb. 1:1,2

It claims to be truthful and factual and is accepted as such by Christians. Many other religions also claim revelations from this same source.

2. SATAN AND HIS ANGELS:

> "...Satan himself is transformed into an angel of light. Therefore it is no great thing if his ministers also be transformed as the ministers of righteousness...." II Cor. 11:14-15

Satan and His angels (evil spirits) do not come to us loudly announcing that they are satanic and evil. They disguise themselves as angels of light sent from God with a message from Him. They pretend to speak truth but actually speak lies to deceive man.

3. NEUROSIS:

Extremely neurotic individuals imagine themselves to be Christ, Napoleon, or some other famous figure. They see and hear various people and events that seem real to them but actually are only figments of their neurotic minds. The revelations that these individuals receive, though evil spirits may also be involved, are real to them. There is no intent to deceive. In their minds they are actually seeing and hearing the events they describe.

4. DRUGS:

The American Indians have long used a drug (peote) taken from cactus plants to induce trances in which they commune with the spiritual realm and receive guidance and revelation. The Chinese have long used opium for the same purpose. The drug culture of our time has also produced a large group of individuals who use drugs to commune with spirits.

5. SELF-DECEPTION and HYPNOTISM:

From ancient times, certain individuals have been used by kings and leaders to receive revelations concerning a future battle or some other future event. Through self-induced spells and hypnotic trances, they receive various revelations. Here again, evil spirits may be involved, but often it is only the activity of their own minds or the power of suggestion.

Some contemporary psychiatrists have induced adults to recall supposed sexual abuse by parents when they were small children. The psychiatrist and the patients, as they listen to the events supposedly flowing out of the subconscious mind, believe the events actually happened. Other psychiatrists have found that these supposed events never happened but have come from the power of suggestion by the psychiatrist.

6. PURPOSEFUL FRAUD:

Riches and recognition can be gained from religion. This aspect has attracted many individuals to proclaim their own teachings disguised as a new religion. The heart of these religions is usually borrowed from existing religions such as Christianity or Buddhism with the addition of some teachings from the founder. Charismatic individuals attract a following, collect money, and succeed in becoming rich and gaining recognition. Many who start such religions do not even believe their own teaching.

Almost all of the thousands of religions in the world have come through these six sources of revelations. Each is BELIEVED by a certain portion of mankind. Thus, FAITH is a necessity for all mankind because all of us live in a house (the universe) that furnishes no specific answers concerning what exists outside our realm or even if there is an outside realm. Even the atheist needs faith. He BELIEVES there is no God and no spiritual realm.

Chapter 11

CATEGORIES OF RELIGIONS

Since all religions are based on faith, we need to distinguish between the two existing types of faith.

FAITH

1. **Subjective:**   blind, superstitious faith based on little or no objective evidence.
2. **Objective:** scientific, logical faith based on evidence (conclusion)

Many people believe that religions are basically saying the same thing. There is a measure of truth in that statement when it comes to moral teaching (man's relationship to man). Most religions teach that you should not kill, steal, commit adultery, lie and deceive, etc. Most also teach that you should be kind, show love, mercy, forgiveness, etc. In the moral realm, they are similar.

When it comes to the spiritual realm, however, they are hopelessly at odds. The span of teachings stretch from no god to many gods; from no life after death to eternal life after death; from salvation for a few to salvation for all; from the survival of the individual after death to the annihilation of the individual; from denial of a satanic kingdom to the recognition of such; etc. Though religions in the moral realm are very similar, they certainly are not saying the same thing about the unknown spiritual realm. All cannot be right.

How can we separate truth from error? Most people believe that since religions speak mainly of the spiritual realm, there is no real way. There is, however, one course of action open to us. We can use our logic and the principles of scientific investigation to distinguish fact from fantasy. To take any other course of action is to revert to "blind faith," speculation, and unfounded hope.

In the physical realm, throughout history mankind has believed many false theories concerning life, the world, the universe, the sun, and geography. Mankind has separated truth from error, fact from superstition, and reality from myth, by strictly following the basic principles of scientific investigation, discussed previously.

Only by adhering to these very same principles can truth be separated from error in the spiritual realm. God gave us minds to use in testing these conflicting claims, so first, let us divide the religions of the world into three broad categories:

1. Those that speak only of the spiritual realm.
2. Those that speak mainly of the spiritual realm and only briefly or inaccurately concerning the real world that we live in.
3. Those that speak in great detail concerning both realms.

Next, even though we can't enter the spiritual realm to examine it, let us test the revelations that supposedly come from that realm for objective evidence.

1. Those religions that speak only of the spiritual realm—

Buddhism, Shintoism, animism, New Age, and many others--fall into this category. In Japan I once had occasion to compare with a Buddhist scholar the teachings of Christianity and Buddhism. After comparing the teachings of both, I asked that we also compare the objective evidence that supports each. He answered that Buddhism does not rest on evidence.

Since religions of this type do not rest on objective evidence, how do they command faith? They rely mainly on subjective experiences and on phenomena from the spiritual realm to convince followers:

* *Miracles*
* *Miraculous healing*
* *Answered prayer*
* *Prophetic utterances*
* *Spiritual experiences*
* *Testimony of personal blessing*

Since almost all religions, including Christianity, can testify of these spiritual happenings, they are of little help in distinguishing which religion is speaking truth. All these experiences are subjective and therefore offer little objective evidence for testing. God is capable of doing all these things--so is Satan.

The powers that operate in the spiritual realm, both good and evil, are much stronger and wiser than we are. Just as an adult can easily deceive a five-year-old child into believing in Santa Claus and almost anything else, evil spirits through various spiritual manifestations can make us believe that we are receiving truth from the spiritual realm. These spirits can claim to be Jesus Christ, Buddha, Mohammed or anyone else and tell us anything that they desire. We have no way of testing these claims OBJECTIVELY; we are like babes in the woods.

These spiritual encounters are real. Those experiencing them are actually hearing and seeing. The question remains, however, are they being told and shown truth or lies concerning the spiritual world? There is no way of testing OBJECTIVELY; they can only believe blindly and hope that what they are experiencing and learning is truth.

> 2. **Those religions that speak mainly of the spiritual realm and only briefly (many times inaccurately) concerning the world that we live in—**

Of the world's major religions, Islam and Hinduism would fall into this category. Both speak of actual historical events, but only briefly (or inaccurately in the case of Hinduism). Neither offers much that can be tested objectively by rules governing scientific investigation. Biblical influence in Islam is, of course, strong but the historical portions of the writings of Mohammed cover only a brief period of time--mainly his life. The rest of the Koran primarily concerns revelations from the spiritual realm.

3. Those religions that speak in great detail concerning both realms--

Only the Bible speaks in great detail concerning both the earthly and heavenly realms. We can test the teachings of the Bible concerning our world.   If it speaks accurately about this world, then we have grounds to believe that it probably speaks accurately about the spiritual realm.

Mormonism, for example, also claims to speak truthfully regarding both realms, as their "Book of Mormon" (supposedly miraculously translated from plates found in New York State) purports to tell the history of the early Americas. It supposedly tells about actual people who lived here, real events, real wars, and real cities.

Not one of these tribes, events or cities, however, has ever been discovered by historians or archaeologists. In relating the history of the early Americas, the "Book of Mormon" never mentions the Aztecs, Mayas, etc. Its basic story is not confirmed by scientific research, so no modern historian or archaeologist ever refers to the "Book of Mormon" to gain insight into pre-Columbian American history. How different from the Bible where literally thousands of names of places, peoples, events, etc. have been amply verified as being extremely accurate!

Probably as much as 70% of the Bible speaks directly or indirectly concerning our world. It is basically the history of mankind from the very beginning to the very end of our world. It especially follows the people of every generation who believe in a Creator God as they walk through the pages of history from the Mesopotamian Valley all the way to 100 A.D., the close of the New Testament.

The Bible is talking about real history, real geography, real people, real events, real wars, real towns, and real rulers. It speaks accurately of the distant past and, through prophecy, of events taking place at the present time and into the distant future. Because it has been proven to speak accurately concerning past events and people, it commands the respect of historians and archaeologists the world over. They use it as a reference book in investigating these ancient happenings.

There are, of course, problems and seeming contradictions existing between these disciplines and the Biblical record. Continuing investigation and discovery have, however, gradually resolved many of these difficulties. The field of investigation covers more than 4,000 years of events occurring over extensive areas in three continents, so unresolved problems will certainly exist. Further study will continue to resolve some of these problems.

As stated previously, if man-made systems and nature's systems were placed on a scale of 1 to 100 in order of complexity, man-made systems would barely occupy the first digit, while the systems in nature would all fall between 90 and 100. This evidence demands faith in a creator God.

Likewise, if we placed the religions of the world on the same scale based on the amount of objective evidence supporting them, we would find that Christianity would be 100 and all of the rest would range from 1 to 10. This objective evidence demands faith in the Bible alone.

Scientifically speaking, based on the evidence of accuracy in the realm that we can test, we have grounds to "conclude" that the Bible (God's revelation to man) is trustworthy in the realm that we cannot test. This is the basis of Christian faith. This is the step of faith that the Bible asks followers to take. This is the same methodology that scientists through the ages have employed as they have investigated the unknown.

There is no other religion in the world that can compare with the abundant objective evidence offered by the Bible. Instead of comparing teaching with teaching, we should be comparing evidence with evidence. If all mankind would stop believing blindly and draw conclusions only from the evidence, the Bible alone would remain as believable. Simply stated, the basic difference between Christianity and the religions of the world is OBJECTIVE EVIDENCE. Christianity stands head and shoulders above all other religions in this realm.

Three of the great religions of the world claim to flow from the Bible--Judaism, Christianity, and Islam. All three obtain their legitimacy from the Bible. Without this basis, they would lack objective evidence as support. How do they differ from Christianity?

ISLAM, while claiming to stem from the Old Testament, is really based on the Koran written by Mohammed, their prophet. The Koran tells of Mohammed's life--His wars, His wives, and events of the time. These portions are historical and serve as evidence to support His actual existence.

Almost all other portions pertain to moral and spiritual teachings with little evidence to command belief. We can also compare the teachings of Mohammed with the teachings of the Old Testament and the New Testament in reaching a conclusion concerning the truth of these teachings. We will find that Mohammed's teachings contradict the Bible. The objective evidence supporting the Koran is also scant in comparison. Only Christianity remains believable BASED ON THE EVIDENCE.

JUDAISM believes the same Old Testament as Christians do and, therefore, rests on objective evidence. However, it rejects the New Testament and the Messiahship of Jesus. In deciding which to believe, since both rest on the Old Testament, we are limited to a study of the teachings and prophecies of the Old Testament concerning the Messiah and a study of the life of Christ and its objective evidence. An objective study of these two topics will leave only Christianity as believable BASED ON THE EVIDENCE.

In conclusion: The Bible claims to be a revelation from the Creator to man.

> "...Eye hath not seen, nor ear heard, neither have entered into the heart of man, the things which God hath prepared for them that love Him, but <u>God hath revealed them unto us by His Spirit...</u>" (I Cor. 2:9,10).

This gives every evidence of being true. Therefore, we believe what the Bible teaches concerning spiritual things and reject those teachings from other religions contradicting the Bible. Because it came from God, the Bible becomes our standard for separating truth from error. It gives detailed and clear answers to the major questions of all mankind.   It tells us:

- **Who God is**
- **Why God made us**
- **Where we are going**
- **How we can live with God forever**
- **The history of believers from the beginning**
- **About life after death**

- **About the spiritual realm**
- **Where evil came from**
- **The ultimate eradication of evil**
- **The end of all things**

These explanations ring true. They are logical and clear. We can thus conclude that the Creator of the universe has actually given us a trustworthy revelation by which we can know that which can be known only by REVELATION.

Many books have been written on the evidence supporting the Bible (Note Bibliography) so that we will not duplicate what is already available in books written by specialists in the various fields of learning that the Bible touches.

Since the Bible speaks about the real world, it touches on almost every field of learning--history, geography, archaeology, astronomy, biology, geology, and linguistics--to name a few. Its main purpose, however, is not to teach these subjects but to relate what God wants us to know so that we can live a life that fulfills His purpose in creating us.

> "The secret *things belong* unto the LORD our God, but those *things which*

are revealed *belong* unto us and to our children forever, that *we* may do all the words of this law." Deut. 29:29

The detailed prophecies of the Bible concerning the Jews, Christianity, Christ, and the countries surrounding Palestine are unique in their scope and accuracy--further evidence of the Bible's reliability.

Part III

GOD CAME

(Jesus Christ)

Chapter 12

JESUS THE CHRIST

In approaching this vast subject, I would like first of all to explain the Bible's teaching (both Old and New Testament) concerning Christ. In this explanation I will not seek to verify each point by Scripture references. The appendix will provide references from Scripture to support the interpretation.

Let's go back to Genesis 1, where God invites man to stand with Him on the earth and observe the order of creation as it unfolds around Him. Only, in this context, we do not stand on the earth because the universe has not yet been created. We are standing only with God--at the very beginning before anything was.

We are, in a sense, standing by ourselves and seeing nothing around us. God is there--eternally existing as Father, Son, and Holy Spirit--an absolute being who is invisible to us because He is a spirit.

The very first thing that we would see, if given spiritual eyes to behold, would be Jesus in His glorious Heavenly body--born from the Father--"the first born of all creation." This is not the beginning of Jesus. He has existed eternally as God--without beginning and without end. He stands there now in the form that will accomplish our redemption--the "Lamb slain from the foundation of the world."

In helping Japanese to understand the Bible's teaching concerning Christ, I use water as an illustration. It is not perfect, as no illustration is sufficient to explain the Bible's teaching concerning the God-Head. It is, however, as close as any illustration can be to help us grasp the Bible's teaching concerning God.

Water exists as H-O-H (H_2O) just as the one God eternally exists as Father-Son-Holy Spirit. Just as it is impossible to remove one of the three elements that make up water and still have water, it is impossible to divide the God-Head. God eternally exists as Father, Son, and Holy Spirit. The Holy Spirit by Himself is not the God of the Bible. The Son by Himself is not the God of the Bible. God cannot be divided and still be God. This is the mystery of the God-Head.

Though the Son died on the cross for us, in some sense God Himself--Father, Son, and Holy Spirit--died for us. When Jesus walked the earth for 30 years, He was totally God--Father, Son, and Holy Spirit--and at the same time totally man. This is the mystery of the incarnation.

So if we return to the very beginning and use water to illustrate God, we would be standing alone in the midst of water existing as vapor and thus invisible. If we analyzed the invisible vapor, we would see that it exists eternally as H_2O.

Suddenly water in its liquid form (Christ in His Heavenly form) would appear born, so to speak, out of vapor--born of the Father. This is the first visible thing we would see. We have witnessed the birth (vapor becoming liquid) of the only begotten Son of God--the assumption of the heavenly form that would later, in the flesh, die for the sins of the world.

This is not His beginning because He is the eternal God without beginning. If we analyzed this liquid, we would find that it is composed of H_2O. (Christ in His heavenly form is still entirely God existing as Father-Son-Holy Spirit.)

We would next see the liquid form of God (Christ) speak into existence the heavens and the earth. We would stand in awe (whether it was done in six days or a trillion years) as the whole universe and all that is in it expanded millions of light years. We would see Christ create all that exists on earth. Lastly we would witness the creation of man in Christ's image.

Throughout the Old Testament, we would see Christ in His heavenly form (liquid form) fellowship with Adam and Eve in Eden and appear to Abraham, Moses, Daniel, and many others. We would witness the Holy Spirit, through the prophets, speak into existence the Old Testament containing the abundant prophecies of the coming incarnation (liquid becoming ice).

At the incarnation, we would see the pre-existent Christ implanted by the Holy Spirit into the womb of the virgin Mary as material man (ice, a solid). Jesus is now not a liquid (a heavenly form) but ice (a physical man). We human beings, to expand the water illustration to us, are born as ice (material bodies). After death at our resurrection, we will assume our liquid (heavenly bodies) existence, having bodies like Christ's resurrected body.

As Jesus walked the earth and performed miracles in His ice (bodily) form, He simultaneously existed in His vapor (spirit) form. Water (God) simultaneously existed as ice (Jesus the man) and vapor (God the Father whom He prays to continuously). If we analyzed visible ice and invisible vapor, we would find both composed of the same elements. Thus Jesus was not part of God. He <u>was</u> God, just as ice is water.

God was invisible (vapor) and at the same time visible (ice). The one God existed simultaneously as ice and vapor--both totally water (both totally God). Just as ice does not possess the same properties as does liquid or vapor, Jesus in His humanity possessed all of the limitations that we physical beings have.

At His resurrection, Jesus' body was raised in its liquid (heavenly) form and in this form appeared to the twelve, to many others, and lastly to Paul. In heaven we also, in our liquid forms, will fellowship with God through Christ in His liquid form (heavenly form). The very difficult passage in I Cor. 15: 24-28 may indicate that after all is accomplished according to His original purposes, Jesus will once again revert to His vapor (Spiritual) form,

"that God may be all in all."

In summary, we have witnessed Jesus as vapor, liquid, solid, liquid and finally (perhaps) as vapor once again. In all these forms, He is totally God--without beginning and without ending.

To illustrate the reason for this transformation, I ask, "Can you crush vapor with a hammer?" Vapor cannot be so crushed, but if it is converted into ice, it can be easily crushed. God in His spiritual form could not die on the cross for us, but by assuming a physical form, He could and did. Through Jesus Christ, He has shown His great love for us. The Bible teaches that Jesus was not a substitute for God; He was very God--just as ice is very water.

Therefore Christianity starts with God and ends with God. The God who created is the same God who spoke (the Bible) and is the same God who came. We do not believe in three Gods but in only one who eternally exists as Father-Son-Holy Spirit. Thus the subject of this book--GOD IS; GOD SPOKE; GOD CAME.

The water illustration, though not perfect, helps us to understand. This illustration is also very effective in sharing with Jehovah Witnesses who believe, without any scriptural evidence, that Jesus was created. The Bible states that He was BORN, not created. Anything born is always the same as its parent (ice from vapor).

Japanese naturally look at Jesus as just being the founder of another religion such as Buddha or

Mohammed, as do many Americans. In witnessing to Japanese or anyone else, it is very important that they understand from the beginning that the one creator--God has done everything. Their faith must be established on these three pillars. This more than anything has given stability to my ministry in Japan.

The Bible teaches that we were made in the image of God so that we could walk with Him, fellowship with Him, and work with Him. In our witnessing, we are not attempting to convince people to follow a different religion or a different religious leader. We are just trying to persuade them to do what they were created for--WALK WITH THE GOD WHO IS. This is the duty of all mankind because GOD IS and He created us for this purpose. That is why all mankind has a "religious" nature.

Through the Bible, God has revealed to us His innermost thoughts as they relate to man. To thoroughly understand GOD CAME, we need to take one more step back into eternity--INTO THE VERY MIND OF GOD--and listen as He thinks and plans.

We stood with Him on the earth and watched as He created our environment. In the first part of this chapter, we stepped back and watched Jesus, "the first born of all creation," as He created.

Now, excerpting His thoughts as He revealed them to us in the Bible, we stand, so to speak, in the mind of God before anything was and listen to Him planning the creation of beings made in His image to fellowship with Him.

God, as He contemplates His absoluteness-- absolute love, peace, joy, contentment, satisfaction, fulfillment, and freedom--knows that He Himself can enjoy all that He is forever and forever; or He can create other beings to share in all that He is. (Since we are made in the image of God we, even in our fallen condition, can experience love, joy, and peace in a limited sense.) To experience absolute love, absolute peace, and absolute joy is beyond our comprehension, yet this is what God has planned for us.

So before anything was, He decided to share Himself with others. Just as the makers of all systems first saw in their minds the systems that they would make, God saw in His great mind everything that He would make and everything that would result from this decision. Nothing was hidden from Him because He is God and can see clearly the end from the beginning.

In His mind He knew that if He made creatures truly like Himself, then these creatures would be free, as God Himself is free. True freedom would carry with it the possibility of not following God and thus bring about the introduction of sin. This would result in death, suffering, and ultimately eternal separation from God in Hell. And God, because He is God, not only knew that this would be possible but knew that IT WOULD HAPPEN.

At that point nothing had as yet been made, so God could have decided that since sin, death, and Hell are going to be the result, He would not make man. Why then did He decide to create man, knowing the terrible result? Because there was another solution--to create and then correct man's blunders. He could allow us freely to make the wrong decisions and then CORRECT those mistakes. Corrected (redeemed) man would then be able to live with God and enjoy Him forever just as God desired from the very beginning.

God knew that the unavoidable result of sin would be death--physical, spiritual, and eternal in Hell. He also knew that there would be only one way to correct man, and that would be for someone to take man's punishment for sin--death. He also knew that only one person is big enough to die for all mankind and that is God Himself. Therefore, if God chose to create man, then He would be the only one who could die for man in order to correct and redeem mankind.

God did not have to create man. God was sufficient in Himself without man. Yet His great love led Him to choose to share Himself even at the cost of paying the penalty of death for His created beings. This is love--absolute love. So when He chose to create, He at the same time chose to die--to become the

> "...lamb slain from the foundation of the world." Rev. 13:8.

> "Herein is love, not that we loved God, but that He loved us, and sent His Son *to be* the propitiation for our sins." I Jn. 4:10

We cannot fathom such great love--that the creator of the universe would die for us simple creatures--yet that is what He did. ABSOLUTE LOVE is the only explanation.

With this decision to create beings like Himself, to allow sin and death, came also the decision to die as a substitute for all mankind.

With His magnificent mind, He could see and name every individual who would be born into this world. He knew from eternity those who would be saved and those who would reject His sacrifice for sin. Thus, from eternity He could write in His "Book of Life" all the names of the redeemed. From this knowledge, He could, in His omnipotence, selectively place each individual in the century, in the country, in the race, and in the family that would be best for him or her. We did not choose our sex, our family, country, or century of birth. God made these choices for us.

Before creating anything, God the Son, Jesus, assumed His Heavenly body--the body that would be sacrificed for mankind.

> "...Sacrifice and offering thou wouldest not, but a body hast thou prepared me."
> Heb. 10:5.

Jesus marks the very beginning not only of physical creation but also the very beginning of God's plan of salvation for man. Jesus is not, as Jehovah Witnesses teach, someone created by God to die for us. That would not show God's love, but cowardice.

Jesus is God. Jehovah of the Old Testament is Jesus of the New Testament. Thus the name Jehovah is never found in the Greek manuscripts of the New Testament--only the name, Jesus. He

> "being in the form of God...took upon him the form of a servant, and was made in the likeness of men...he

humbled himself, and became obedient
unto death" (Phil. 2:6-8)

God Himself chose to die for us; so in the words
of the previous illustration, vapor became ice. Herein is
love--unfathomable and absolute!

When Adam and Eve sinned, God was not taken
by surprise. He knew that would happen before He
created them. So after man sinned, God for the first
time began to explain to them His plan of
redemption--His plan to correct this horrible mistake.
He promised

> "...I will put enmity between thee
> (serpent) and the woman...it shall
> bruise thy head...and thou shalt bruise
> his heal." Gen. 3:15

The remainder of the Old Testament reveals the
gradual unfolding and clarification of this plan
conceived in eternity. Through more than 100 specific
prophecies, the time, place, manner, and other specific
details of the coming of the promised Savior are
recorded. His life, death, and resurrection are
prophesied in detail.

The Japanese Bible is entitled "OLD PROMISE"
and "NEW PROMISE" and so clearly emphasizes God's

promise to man. That promise is fulfilled through the coming of Jesus Christ into this world as a seed of the woman. The life and majesty of Jesus the Christ is detailed for us by eye witnesses in the first four books of the New Testament.

Jesus Christ's existence, life, death, and bodily resurrection are fully supported by abundant objective evidence. This evidence is detailed in many scholarly books in all related fields of learning (Note Bibliography). In concluding this section, I will briefly mention some of the evidence that authenticates this life--a life that only God could have lived.

It should be emphasized that there is more objective evidence from the first, second, and third centuries to support the life of Jesus than that of any other contemporary figure--Alexander the Great, Julius Caesar, Cleopatra, etc. Judging from the plentiful manuscriptural, historical, and archaeological evidence, in addition to the eyewitnesses, the life of Jesus cannot be doubted based on lack of evidence.

Because the life of Jesus is filled with miracles, it is doubted and contested. This is only natural because people do not ordinarily raise the dead, heal the sick, walk on water, and bodily rise from the dead. Although such doubt is natural, it springs not from a paucity of evidence but from the inability to believe that the God of creation actually came into this world in the form of man. If He did, then a life such as that recorded of Jesus should be expected.

I consider myself to be a very logical and pragmatic person. I do not find it easy to believe so-called healings, miracles, etc. Yet I find little difficulty in accepting the recorded life of Christ. The reasons for this:

1. The conclusive evidence supporting the existence of God. This is foundational. He actually is. Therefore everything has meaning and purpose. We are here because He made us.

2. The absolute necessity of REVELATION from God if we are ever to know spiritual truth. Logic and science cannot give us these answers because they investigate only the material realm.

3. The Bible's claim to be that revelation and the abundant evidence verifying that claim.

4. The logic of the Bible's principal teaching that God who created us will also redeem us--even at the cost of Himself. Since the

existence of God is proven, this makes sense to me.

5. The more than 100 prophecies in the Old Testament that foretold, hundreds of years before Jesus, the coming of

    "...the everlasting Father...
    the mighty God..."Isaiah 9:6

6. The numerous claims of Jesus, directly and indirectly, to deity.

7. These claims are amply proven by His life and deeds--recorded by eye- witnesses.

8. The bodily resurrection and ascension into heaven are certainly believable of one who <u>came</u> from heaven.

9. The consistent testimony of all New Testament writers to the deity of Christ and to His resurrection.

10. The consistent testimony to the same by the church fathers of the second and third centuries.

11. The preponderance of solid manuscriptural, historical, and archaeological evidence from the first through the third centuries:

a. The records of Jesus' life were written by eyewitnesses who gladly died for what they believed.

b. The entire New Testament was written within 60 years of Christ's death.

c. The writings of the second century church fathers affirm the existence of the New Testament books and their veracity.

d. Over 5,000 major and partial manuscripts of the New Testament from the first through the third centuries have been discovered. The earliest is dated around 125 A.D.

e. The testimony of Josephus, a Jewish historian from the first century.

f. Roman records and writers of the second and third centuries give credence.

g. The change from Saturday to Sunday (the day of Christ's resurrection) as the day for Christians to meet together.

h. The celebration of Easter from earliest times by Christians.

Using supportive, OBJECTIVE EVIDENCE as our basis, if we compare the life of Jesus with that of all other religious leaders by placing them on a scale of 1 to 100, we would find that the religious leaders of the world would occupy only the first few digits and Jesus would be 100.

In comparing books supporting the life of Christ as recorded in the Gospels with those written by authors denying that life, one thing is very evident. Writers supporting the Gospel accounts base their reasoning on all the abundant objective evidence. Writers denying these accounts cannot base their reasoning on comparable evidence from the first two centuries of Christianity;   they have to resort to speculation and arrive at strained conclusions drawn from scarce evidence.   If you read any of these books, look for quotes of objective evidence; you will find few.

IN CONCLUSION

BASED ON THE EVIDENCE,
WE CHRISTIANS BELIEVE:

1. **GOD IS.** He actually exists and is the creator of all that is.
2. **GOD SPOKE.** Through chosen writers, He gave to mankind a revelation, the Bible, filled with truths that can be known only by revelation.
3. **GOD CAME.** The eternal God who created all and who spoke the Bible into existence actually came into this world as Jesus Christ, died for our sins, was buried, and three days later bodily rose from the grave and ascended into heaven where He still reigns as the eternal God.

It is commonly thought that in the realm of religion you can basically believe any religion as long as you are sincere. That type of thinking cannot be applied to any other area of learning. It conveniently dispenses with logic, reason, evidence, and scientific investigation. Apply that thinking to every other field of learning, and you will soon see the absurdity of such.

1. **Mathematics:** You can believe that $2 + 2 = 4$ or 5 or 6 or 7, etc., and as long as you are sincere, it is okay.

2. **Geography:** You can believe that Japan lies off the coast of New York, and as long as you are sincere, it is okay.

3. **Astronomy:** You can believe that the sun rotates around the earth, and as long as you are sincere, it is okay.

4. **Physics:** You can believe that gravity does not exist, and as long as you are sincere, it is okay.

5. **History:** You can believe that Napoleon was a Roman General, and as long as you are sincere, it is okay.

6. Let's apply it to our everyday life:

   a. You can believe that I am a Canadian or an Englishman or an Australian, and as long as you are sincere, it is okay.

   b. You can believe that any airplane you ride will take you to New York, and as long as you are sincere, it is okay.

The fallacy of such reasoning is obvious. In seeking truth, we may find many theories, but there is really only one right answer. The only way that we can find truth is to rely upon our ability to reason, to gather evidence, compare the evidence that supports the various theories, and draw conclusions BASED ON THE EVIDENCE. When we forsake this methodology that has enabled mankind through the centuries to separate truth from error, we subject ourselves to every kind of deception and find that we can believe anything. We can believe any voice that comes from the spiritual realm and any new teaching that springs from the fertile mind of man.

THE CONCEPT, *"YOU CAN BELIEVE WHATEVER YOU WANT; AS LONG AS YOU ARE SINCERE, IT IS OKAY,"* IS APPLICABLE ONLY IF TRUTH IS NOT IMPORTANT.

Religions should be regarded like conflicting scientific theories, because that is exactly what they are--conflicting teachings concerning the spiritual realm. Just as myths, legends, and superstitions having little or no evidence supporting them have been rejected by thinking people throughout the centuries, so religions having little or no supporting objective evidence should be rejected.

Theories that at one time seemed to be supported by sufficient objective evidence were later abandoned as other theories supported by more reliable evidence surfaced. It is, for example, no longer believed that:

> The earth is flat;
> The sun rotates around the earth; and
> The Americas are the East Indies.

Thus, if the religions of the world were all examined by the rules of logic and scientific investigation, only one would remain as believable--Christianity.

A young Japanese college student, a new Christian, once asked me, "What if some religion with greater objective evidence than that which supports Christianity comes along?" I answered, "Believe it." That will never happen, though, because the evidence supporting the Bible begins with creation and continues to the present through fulfilled prophecy and into the future through prophecy to be fulfilled.

Remember, one of the basic rules of scientific investigation is COMPARISON OF EVIDENCE. The gathering of objective evidence is extremely important; however, it is only by COMPARISON of evidence that truth can be separated from error. Since the teachings of the various faiths are basically only theories, we should not be comparing teachings with teachings but EVIDENCE WITH EVIDENCE.

So in the religious realm, WHAT ARE THE ALTERNATIVES? What other religious teaching can even remotely compare with the objective evidence that supports Christianity? All religions can produce abundant SUBJECTIVE evidence--healings, miracles, visions, dreams, and spiritual experiences. But when it comes to the overwhelming objective evidence that supports the basic pillars of Christianity (GOD IS; GOD SPOKE; GOD CAME), none are even viable contenders. That includes atheism, which is just another faith not supported by the evidence.

Christianity, when measured by the proven rules of scientific investigation, remains unique. There are some problems existing in the realm of Bible history, archaeology, and interpretation, but none of these are insurmountable. Many books have been written dealing with these supposed contradictions. In any area of learning, problems and contradictions must be examined. So confronting problems in a subject so vast as that covered by the Bible is certainly not surprising.

It is OBJECTIVE EVIDENCE that sets Christianity apart from the religions of the world. This point cannot be over emphasized.

AN APPEAL

GOD IS. He is living. He is a spirit and is with you as you read this. He is your creator. He loves you and created you to walk with Him forever. He loves you so much that in the person of Christ, He died for your sins in order that you may live with Him now and throughout eternity and that you may enjoy Him and His new creation for ever and ever.

The Bible says:

> "Believe on the Lord Jesus Christ and thou shalt be saved." Acts 16:31

> "Whosoever shall call upon the name of the Lord shall be saved."   Rom.10:13

> "For God so loved the world that He gave His only begotten son, that . whosoever believeth in Him should not

> perish, but have everlasting life." John 3:16

The Bible teaches that:

> "All have sinned and come short of the glory of God." Rom. 3:23

> "There is none righteous, no, not one." Rom. 3:10

Because all have sinned, Christ came into this world and bore the punishment for the sins of us all by His death on the cross. In that terrible cry from the cross,

> "...My God, my God, why hast thou forsaken me?" Mt. 27:46

He actually experienced the eternal punishment due each of us--an infinite one suffering for finite mankind in order that we might be forgiven and live with Him. The punishment for sin (death) has been paid. God does not demand further payment from us. He freely forgives all who ask Him for salvation through Jesus Christ.

In the Old Testament He promised this salvation. All Old Testament believers were forgiven and saved by a faith that believed this promise and looked forward to its fulfillment. We in the New Testament age are forgiven and saved by believing that Jesus Christ fulfilled the promise and by asking God to save us through Jesus Christ. As you read this, if you have never from you heart asked God to forgive your sins through Jesus Christ, do so now. He will cleanse you from all sin and His Holy Spirit will come into your heart to teach and guide you. That same Holy Spirit will be with you throughout every trial of life and take you to heaven to live with your creator forever.

Through the work of the Holy Spirit, He will ultimately correct us and make us the perfect beings that He envisioned in the beginning. In Heaven, we will be like Adam and Eve before sin--perfect. They, however, were innocent with no knowledge of sin. We will be forgiven and perfected sinners whom God has promised will never sin again. We, unlike Adam and Eve, will have a knowledge of the terribleness of sin.

Accept Jesus. Start reading your Bible, and each time you open it, ask God to help you understand it so that you may grow spiritually. Seek out Christian fellowship and take your stand as one of God's children. He has called you not only <u>to walk with Him</u> but also <u>to work with Him</u>. You can best do this through a good

Bible-believing church. Many people are hurting, and we are here to participate in His ministry of compassion and love. God's Holy Spirit will guide you and cause you to grow more and more like Jesus Christ.

APPENDIX

Scriptures Relating to Jesus as Explained in Chapter 11

Jesus, the first born of all creation:
Col. 1:15-20; Jn. 1:1-3; Prov. 8:22-32; Heb. 1:1-14.

Jesus, the creator of everything:
Above scriptures plus, Jn. 1:10; I Cor. 8:6; Rev. 3:14. (The source of God's creation.)

Jesus is God: Direct statements:
Isa. 9:6; Jn. 1:1 & 18; Jn. 20:28; Heb. 1:8; I Jn. 5:20. Indirect statements; Jn. 10:30; 14:9; Acts 20:28; Phil. 2:5-11; Col. 2:9,10; I Tim. 3:15,16; Titus 2:13; Heb. 1:6 & 8; II Pet. 1:1

Jesus, His Old Testament appearances:
Gen. 3:8; 18:1-33; Ex. 24:9-11; 33:18-23; Dan. 3:23-25; 7:9-14; Jn. 8:56-59; I Cor. 10:4 and many more passages that probably refer to Christ.

Old Testament prophecies of Christ:
Gen. 3:15; 49:10; Num. 24:15-19; Dt. 18:18,19; Job 19:25-27; Psa. 2:12; 22:10-22; Prov. 30:4; Isa. 7:14; 9:6,7; 53:1-12; Dan. 9:24-27; 12:1; Mic.: 4:2,3; Zech. 9:9; 12:8-12; 14:1-9; Mal. 3:1-3; 4:5,6.

Jesus, God incarnate:
Mt. 1:18-25; Lk. 1:26-38; Jn. 1:14; Phil. 2:5-11; I Tim. 3:15,16.

Jesus, His resurrection and ascension:
Psa. 16:10,11; Mt. 28; Mk. 16; Lk. 24; Jn. 20 & 21; Acts. 1:1-14; 22-36; 3:11-16; 4:1-12; 5:27-32; I Cor. 15:1-19 and many others.

Jesus, His present reign in Heaven:
I Cor. 15:25; Eph. 1:18-23; Phil. 2:9-11; Col. 3:1; Heb. 1:3, 4:14-16, 5:1-10, 7:24-28; 9:11,12; and others.

Jesus, His final destiny:
I Cor. 15:22-28; Rev. 21:1-8; 22-27; 22:1-5, 13-15.

GLOSSARY

Agnostic   one who doubts the existence of God but neither affirms nor denies it

Animate   anything that is living

Apologetics   a study of the evidences that support the Bible

Atheist   one who denies the existence of God

Attributes of God   character of God

Buddhist   one who follows the teaching of Buddhism

Discipline   a field of study such as biology or geography.

Entropy   the tendency of all things in the universe to deteriorate, slow down, move from complexity to simplicity, decay, lose energy, etc.

Firmament   sky

Inanimate   non-living, anything not living (a corpse is inanimate but organic)

Incarnation   to be in body form, in the form of a human

Inorganic   not from living matter, elements not of carbon

Macro   great, large, massive

Objective   factual, real, actual, without bias or prejudice

Organic   from living matter, containing the carbon element

Pantheist   one who believes that nature is god and god is nature

Pragmatic   practical; one who accepts things as they are; a realist

Primate   ape, gorilla, chimpanzee

Shintoist   a believer in the native Japanese religion of Shinto (god's way) that teaches that spirits inhabit all things and must be petitioned and appeased

Subjective   of one's feelings, experiences, emotions

Theist   one who believes in God

Transcendent

separate from; not part of; a transcendent God is not part of His creation; opposite from pantheism

REFERENCE WORKS

Bruce, F. F. *The New Testament Documents: Are They Reliable?* Grand Rapids, MI, Eerdmans 1960. Manuscriptural evidences that give authenticity and authority to the New Testament. 120p.

Bruce, F. F. *The Books and the Parchments*, Rev. ed. Grand Rapids, MI, Eerdmans. A study of the documents underlying the New Testament. 286p.

Campbell, Dr. William. *The QUR'AN and the BIBLE*. (Available through Hugh Ross below). Very detailed, technical, and thorough--written by a competent scholar comparing the two books historically and scientifically. He also compares Mohammed & Christ. Excellent.

Denton, Michael. *Evolution: A Theory in Crisis*. Adler and Adler, Publishers, Inc., 1986, Bethesda, MD. Problems of Darwinian evolution from a purely scientific point of view. Technical but very good.

Filby, F. A. *Creation Revealed*. Fleming H. Revell Co. 1965. An excellent treatise on Genesis 1 as it relates to modern science and an ancient earth. 158p.

Finegan, Jack. *Light from the Ancient Past*. Princeton University Press, 1959, Princeton, NJ. The archeological background of Judaism and Christianity. An excellent textbook for college students. Thorough, but difficult reading. 638p.

Fraser, Gordon H. *Is Mormonism Christian?* Moody Press, Chicago, 1965. A comparison of Mormonism with Christianity--easy reading. 122p.

Gosse, Philip Henry. *Omphalos: An Attempt to Untie the Geological Knot.* London: John Van voorst, Peternoster Row, 1857. One of the earliest books advocating a "finished" creation in six literal days but having an appearance of age.

Green, Michael. *Running From Reality.* Downers Grove, IL, Intervarsity Press, 1983. An excellent, easy reading book showing that the world (not Christians) is running away from the evidence supporting God, the Bible, and Christ. 126p.

Johnson, Philip E. *Darwin on Trial.* Downers Grove, IL, Intervarsity Press by special arrangement with Regnery Gateway, Inc., Washington, DC. A legal expert examines Darwinian evolution through many scientific disciplines and finds it lacking. One of the most recent and effective challenges to orthodox evolutionary thought. 220p.

Josephus, Flavius. *Complete Works.* Translated by William Whiston. Foreword by William Sanford LaSor. Grand Rapids, MI. Kregel Publications, c1981. History of the Jews to 73 A.D. Interesting reading but listed here only because of brief references to Jesus & to John the Baptist. 775p.

Laidlaw, Robert A. *The Reason Why*. Grand Rapids, MI. Zondervan, 1970. A small booklet that logically presents evidence for God and the Bible, closing with a Gospel presentation. 64p.

Lewis, C. S. *Mere Christianity*. New York, Macmillan, 1952. An excellent, logical presentation of the evidence supporting Christianity. 175p.

Lewis, C. S. *The Case for Christianity*. New York, Macmillan, 1952. A well thought out, logical defense of Christianity and its supporting evidence.

McDowell, Josh. and Bill Wilson. *He Walked Among Us*. San Bernardino, CA; Here's Life Publishers, c1988. Evidence for the Biblical Jesus. Thoroughly documented. 366p.

McDowell, Josh. *Evidence That Demands a Verdict,* Rev. ed. San Bernardino, CA, Here's Life Publishers, c1979. Historical evidence for the Christian faith with excellent material for answering the critic. Every informed Christian should have a copy. 387p.

McDowell, Josh. *More Evidence That Demands a Verdict,* Rev. ed. San Bernardino, CA. Here's Life Publishers, c1981. Historical evidences for the

Christian Scriptures. Very technical and detailed in defending Christianity against the claims of higher criticism. 389p.

McDowell, Josh. *More than a Carpenter*. Wheaton, IL; Tyndale House Publishers, 1977. Easy reading defense of the Biblical Jesus. Logical and well suited to give to the non- Christian. 128p.

McDowell, Josh. and John Gilchrist. *The Islam Debate*. San Bernardino, CA; Campus Crusade for Christ, Here's Life Publishers, 1983. A defense of Christianity against Islam from the viewpoint of evidence--quite technical. 199p.

Morris, Henry Madison. *Biblical Creationism*. Henry M. Morris. Grand Rapids, MI, Baker, c1993. What various books of the Bible teach about creation and the flood from a young earth point of view. 276p.

Pentecost, J. Dwight. *Things to Come*. Grand Rapids, MI, Zondervan, 1958. A study in Biblical eschatology. Very thorough and systematic treatment of the great themes of prophecy from a dispensational point of view. 633p.

Ramm, Bernard. *The Christian View of Science and Scripture*. Grand Rapids, MI, Eerdmans, 1955. An attempt to reconcile the Bible's teaching on creation and the flood with present scientific thought.

Ross, Hugh Norman. *Creation and Time.* Colorado Springs, CO, NavPress, 1994. An anti-evolutionary perspective on the creation-date controversy from the viewpoint of a several billion year universe. Very readable. 187p.

Ross, Hugh Norman. *The Creator and the Cosmos.* Colorado Springs, CO; NavPress, 1993. How one of the greatest astronomical discoveries in recent decades reveals the existence of God. 185p.

Tenney, Merrill Chapin, *The Reality of the Resurrection.* Chicago, IL; Moody Press c1963, 1972. A very thorough presentation of the evidences supporting the resurrection of Jesus. 221p.

Whitcomb, John Clement; *The World That Perished.* Grand Rapids, MI; Baker Book House, 1988. 2nd ed. An explanation of the Biblical flood and the fossil record--from a young earth perspective. 178p.

Whitcomb, Jr., John Clement and Henry M. Morris. *The Genesis Flood.* Philadelphia, PA; Presbyterian and Reformed Pub. Co., 1961. The Biblical record of the flood and its scientific implications from a young earth perspective--very thorough. 518p.

Wilder-Smith, A. E. *Man's Origin, Man's Destiny.* Bethany Fellowship, Inc. 1975. Explanation of the defects of evolution from a purely scientific point of view by a qualified Christian scientist. 320p.